ANGLER'S MAIL

HOW TO SUCCEED AT
COARSE
FISHING

HOW TO SUCCEED AT

COARSE FISHING

DAVE COSTER

Consultant Editor: Roy Westwood

HAMLYN

All photographs by Roy Westwood

First published in Great Britain in 1994
by Hamlyn
an imprint of Reed Consumer Books Limited
Michelin House, 81 Fulham Road,
London SW3 6RB
and Auckland, Melbourne, Singapore and Toronto

ISBN 0 600 58505 0

A catalogue record for this book is available from the British Library

Printed in Spain

CONTENTS

Rewards and Opportunities

Take up coarse fishing and you're normally hooked for life. Many millions of anglers will testify to that fact but ask them to explain the chief reason for their compulsion and you'll receive as many answers as there are rivers.

One of the major attractions must be the mystery element. Wherever you fish, another world lies beneath the surface and it's impossible to predict what might come along next.

But the magnetism of fishing does not simply stem from its unpredictability. The thrill of a good fish streaking off with your bait, the sudden arc of the rod, the resultant thump which transmits into your hands, this is an experience not to be missed!

Angling in any of its multiple forms has an uncanny knack of heightening the senses. It could be that unseen quarry attached to your line, or just the feeling of expectation as a float is towed away into the depths. Whatever the cause, it most definitely grips your imagination to the exclusion of everything else. No wonder many anglers admit they experience a marvellous sense of peace while sitting at the waterside.

There are still many unspoilt areas of the country where coarse fishing will undoubtedly take you, but even industrialised areas of canal and river possess their own particular magic. No matter where you go coarse fishing, it will always give you time to reflect and that's surely a benefit worth seeking when most of us live and work in the fast lane.

The beauty of coarse fishing is that it remains relatively inexpensive for newcomers. There are certain junior fishing kits on the market for under £20 which include enough gear to give a flavour of the sport...and to catch that all important first fish.

But a more realistic estimate for a basic starter outfit would be around £100. There's enough good budget tackle around nowadays to be able to test the water, before committing yourself too heavily.

Once you have got yourself kitted out, it shouldn't prove too difficult to find some good fishing. Numerous commercially run, small stillwaters have opened in recent seasons. They are often highly stocked and for the price of a day ticket, offer the beginner a great chance of bagging a big fish – or good catches of smaller ones.

Then there are many hundreds of prolific and well managed club waters, where you don't necessarily have to be an expert to catch some fish.

Once on the bank, the first major challenge to confront any angler, whether novice, or highly experienced, is how to approach and make the best of the swim.

There are numerous critical decisions to take including choice of suitable tackle, baits and methods and the need to identify which part of the swim should be concentrated on. As experi-

ence is gained, this task becomes slightly easier, but the answers are never cut and dried.

Water and weather conditions are constantly changing and a successful formula one day may fail miserably the next.

All this is part and parcel of the sport, a fascinating aspect in fact, which is another reason why anglers are held spellbound all their lives.

SEPARATE GROUPS WITHIN THE SPORT

Coarse fishing embraces several quite distinct categories of angler. The majority are pleasure anglers, who basically go out for their own enjoyment, either individually or in company. Many become very proficient, and sometimes progress into the more competitive spheres of the sport.

Club anglers usually go on regular group outings to a variety of waters. A more competitive aspect enters here. There are often small sweepstakes with cash prizes for the anglers taking the heaviest catches. And, at the end of the season, trophies may be awarded for the top specimen fish, biggest catches and the most consistent points scorers.

Club fishing offers various social functions and regular meetings. It's a very good way for the beginner to learn quickly.

Matchmen often emerge direct from the club scene. Competitive angling has become very professional and some of the top performers are almost making a living from their match winnings. Sponsorship deals from tackle companies may also be involved.

A mature Hertfordshire gravel pit dug during the Second World War to build fighter plane runways. The coloured water suggests there's a good stock of bottom stirring feeders like carp and bream.

Quivertipping on the tidal Yare in Norfolk. The rod is raised high to keep as much of the line as possible clear of the strong flow.

Match fishing revolves around team events and Open competitions for individuals. Team fishing is extremely popular and there are many leagues, including National Championship Divisions and the *Angler's Mail* Super League series. Open matches are listed every week in the *Mail* and offer a unique opportunity for even the raw beginner to line up alongside leading international stars.

Specialists, or specimen hunters as they are commonly called, are dedicated to the pursuit of specimen-sized fish, most notably carp, pike and barbel. These anglers might set themselves tough personal targets and some spend months in search of a specific, known fish.

Heavyweight carp are the most popular species for the majority of specimen anglers. The capture of one fish may entail many hours, even weeks, camped out by the waterside.

CHOOSING A VENUE

There's a vast network of gravel pits and lakes available to the coarse angler along with thousands of miles along rivers and canals. Local clubs and associations control much of this fishing and they issue season or day tickets. There are also private syndicate waters where membership and access is restricted and, at the other extreme, commercially-run complexes where the

FIRST BUY A ROD LICENCE

All anglers aged 12 and over must purchase a rod licence issued by the National Rivers Authority. A single national licence covers the entire country but does not actually confer the right to fish anywhere. Very few stretches of water are free and you'll normally have to buy a day or season ticket in addition to the national rod licence.

The cost of the rod licence has been the subject of fierce debate but there are concessions for anglers aged 12-16, the registered disabled and senior citizens. The licence is valid for two rods

The rod licence helps pay for fisheries work carried out by the National Rivers Authority.

when fishing for coarse fish or eels.

The coarse fishing season runs from June 16 to March 14 although many enclosed stillwaters have traditionally offered all-year-round sport, but only where local byelaws permit the relax-

ation. These laws are now under review.

The principle reasons for maintenance of the Close Season are protection for spawning fish and other wildlife through the Spring. But the need for this protection has long been the source of dispute and fish frequently spawn in the opening months of the season.

The Close Season will probably always stay in force on rivers but stillwaters are sure to remain a bone of contention whatever the NRA decrees.

Boats limit sport on canals in high summer but it's still possible to catch fish between the traffic.

accent is very much on accessibility for all-comers.

Choosing a venue can start within the pages of *Angler's Mail* itself and the Where to Fish feature which describes the location and potential of day ticket venues throughout the UK. The local tackle shop is also a very good source of information and many sell tickets and club books for nearby venues.

Where day tickets are sold, they might be obtainable from a bailiff on the bank, or sometimes in advance from a tackle shop, post office, or private address. Most publicity about waters, explains which procedure is required and sometimes the signboards at fishery entrances explain how and where to buy tickets.

Where season permits, or club books are needed, you may have to apply in advance, but it's not normally a particularly complicated process and generally membership details are well publicised.

Day tickets cost on average from £2 to £5. There are usually concessionary rates for half day, or evening visits, and special rates for children, the disabled and senior citizens.

Season tickets are well worth considering if you intend to fish a particular venue frequently. They can work out much cheaper in the long run, often costing between £10 and £30 for at least nine months' fishing.

Membership of large angling associations like London AA and Birmingham AA, will open up more venues than you could possibly cover in the space of a year.

Another option is to join a commercial fishery group. A good example in the South East area is Leisure Sport, who offer a tremendous choice of gravel pit fisheries for a relatively modest annual outlay.

Some specialist waters are run on a syndicate basis. This prevents too many anglers flooding onto the venue, but can be an expensive option and sometimes there's a long waiting list to join.

Different types of venues can produce different species and the fish may also have very diverse feeding habits from one water to the next. The beginner will do well to note that the skill factor also varies in catching these fish, even when the same species are present in varied types of water.

Rivers may hold species normally associated with running water, such as barbel, chub and dace. But they often also hold more widely distributed fish like roach, bream and carp. Canals are often linked to rivers and it's not unusual to find large colonies of river fish like chub and dace living in them. Just as commonly canal venues

The unmistakable perch with its sharp dorsal spines.

MORE BITES IN SUMMER

The changing seasons have a bearing on how fisheries perform. In the warmer summer months, higher water temperatures make the fish considerably more active. It's easier to tempt bites and to draw fish with liberal amounts of feed.

When the fish are feeding well at these times, the angler can often get away with less finesse in both his tackle and feeding technique. Fish will often take baits up in the water, or even on the surface.

Good catches are still possible in winter, but with much lower water temperatures, the fish are sometimes very lethargic and may be tightly shoaled in their cold weather quarters. Some species only feed for short periods when water temperatures rise by a degree or two.

Now the angler must be very precise and careful with his feed and scale down the tackle and bait size to gain bites in the cold water. Static, bottom presented baits may be the only way to tempt a response.

will hold good stocks of roach, gudgeon, perch, tench, bream and carp.

Common species you'd expect to find in stillwaters are roach, perch, tench, carp, bream and pike. But the boom in highly stocked commercial lake fisheries has led to the introduction of more exotic fish like koi and ghost carp, golden and blue orfe and golden tench. Even experiments involving out and out river species like barbel have had some successes in enclosed lakes.

PICKING THE FIRST ROD

Great care is required, even when selecting a basic starter kit. Cheap rods are only really designed for the holiday maker and merely scratch the sport's potential. Telescopic rods are

Carbon match rod fitted with durable lined rings.

a good example. They might pack into a suitcase for a trip abroad, but they are normally on the short side and rather lacking in casting action.

The best starting point for someone wanting to coarse fish with float tackle is to choose a three-piece, carbon composite rod of at least 12 feet in length. These are often called match rods. There's plenty of good models in the £30 to £40 category and you will soon discover the extra length makes life a lot easier when casting out and retrieving the tackle.

The softer, more forgiving action of a match rod allows you to use realistic tackle on venues where the fish may be shy and require a lighter approach.

It's a good idea for younger anglers to start with a float fishing kit. The only modification here might be determined by the length of rod they can physically hold. But settle for a reasonable length, at least ten feet. It's also preferable to get a three-piece, rather than a telescopic, or two-piece model.

Cheaper kids' fishing kits, which come complete with rod, reel and some accessories, may contain a three-piece solid glass rod and these are passable. Two piece, solid rods are too short, have large eyes and are really meant for spinning. Avoid them if float fishing is the objective.

At the cheaper end of the market, rod blanks are usually made from a composite of glass and carbon. More expensive rods have a higher carbon content.

At the top end of the price range, high carbon rods are extremely light and incredibly thin. Don't let this fool you! They are surprisingly strong, have very fast actions and cost between £90 and £400.

Float rods tend to be three-piece and feature a gentle progression of between ten and 15 line guides or rings down to their tips. They're generally made in lengths between 11 and 14 feet.

Legering, or quivertip rods often start as two-piece blanks in their shorter ten feet lengths. These may look similar, or even double up as short float fishing rods. But they can be singled out by the tip ring which usually has a screw fitting. This enables a quivertip, or swingtip bite indicator to be fitted.

Other quivertip rods have a much thinner tip section, which is spliced-in, with tiny line guides – fitted quite close together. These models often feature brightly painted tips, because this is the part of the rod which shows up bites.

More expensive legering, or feeder rods may be three-piece and can go up to 13 feet in length for long range fishing. These normally have several inter-changeable quivertips, which plug into the blank proper. Multi-tip rods start at around £50 and go up to about £150. They are very versatile. The tips in most makes also fit other multi-tip rods, so a single design's capabilities can be further enhanced.

Browsing over the rod racks in a tackle shop you will notice slight gaps where the sections come together on some assembled rods. This will be seen on spigot joint models and isn't a fault!

The lower section is spigotted and fits inside the next section up. The slight gap is to allow for wear and tear and stops the sections from working loose under the stress of casting.

The overfit joint system is also common. Here the upper section of rod fits snugly over the very gradual taper of the next section down. There is no spigot and this tends to make for slightly softer actioned blanks. Sometimes with this type of rod the tip section slots over the middle piece in the same fashion. But there are also designs where the tip piece can actually push into the next section down.

Basic Actions

Match, or float fishing rods have two main actions. Tip action means the blank is stiffish,

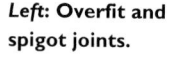

Above: Feeder rod featuring inter-changeable quivertips which are stored inside the handle when not plugged into position.

Left: Overfit and spigot joints.

but has a fine, softer tip. This type of model is often favoured for river fishing where top and bottom attached floats, like sticks, balsas and Avons are used.

In order to get such a forgiving tip – which allows the use of fine lines – a short length of finer solid carbon is often spliced into the tip section of the blank. The strike is often to the side,

Tip Action – usually spliced tip – is favoured for stick and balsa fishing on rivers.
Through Action – usually hollow tip – is ideal for long range work with wagglers.

or slightly upwards with tip actioned rods. Their fast actions are designed to lift line cleanly off the surface.

Through actioned rods rarely have a splice, unless they are very soft and short like some specialist canal models. They generally have hollow tips and bend gradually throughout their length when put under pressure.

These designs are used for long range fishing with waggler, or bottom-end attached floats. Less effort is required to set the hook. Often, the strike is low and less hurried, leaning the rod into a taking fish.

Rings and Handles

A factor which helps to determine rod price is the type of line guide, or ring the manufacturer whips to the blank.

Cheap rods often have chrome guides. They will stand up to a fair bit of use, but will eventually need replacing. Ceramic lined guides have a much greater life span and they cause far less friction on the line as it travels through them. These should last several years.

There are also very streamlined, one-legged, models which suit ultra thin, carbon float rods. They won't detract from the rod's action in any way at all.

Silicone carbide guides are the most expensive and hard wearing. They are only to be found on top of the range specimen, match and feeder rod designs. These may up the price of the rod dramatically, but it should be remembered that they will probably never need replacing.

Most rod handles are still covered in cork, but you will also find some companies experimenting with synthetic rubber handles, or a combination of both materials. Rubber, or Duplon handles have received a mixed reception. This material is now mainly to be found on split handled specimen rods and as an end grip on certain top range match rods.

Standard reel fittings consist of two collars which lock the reel onto the handle. It's best to check these provide adequate security. Some cheaper rods have alloy fittings which tend to work loose while fishing. Plastic and graphite fittings are better formed and generally help the reel to sit more snugly and comfortably on the rod handle.

Some top flight float rods now have screw-in reel fittings, where the upper part of the handle tightens down onto the foot of the reel. These are very secure.

Most split handled specimen rods also have screw fittings to keep the reel from working loose during long casts.

Reel Choices

Fixed Spool Three types of reel are commonly used in coarse fishing. The most popular is the fixed spool. This design has an open face, exposing the line spool. It is probably the best, least complicated reel for a beginner.

Once the bail arm is opened, line flows out unhindered on the cast. Greater distances are achieved and there are rarely any problems with the line bedding in on the spool.

The only drawback with open-faced models occurs when fishing into a facing wind. The line does have a tendency to billow back and tangle around the bail arm mechanism.

Test Curves

Test curve readings are rarely applied to match style rods - their fine tips would have pretty minimal readings anyway.

They are really only relevant for rods which are used to cast heavier weights over greater distances. Some specialist feeder rods do now give a casting weight guide.

But test curves are more in the domain of specimen rods, where carp anglers particularly, think nothing of punching out a bait 100 yards.

The test curve of a blank is gauged by pulling the tip of the rod down into a 45 degree angle with a spring balance. Typical specimen rods will give readings of 1 lb to 3 lb.

The test curve is used as a rough guide to judge the casting weights the rods will comfortably handle. The common equation here is to relate poundage of test curve into casting ounces.

Therefore a 2 lb test rod should be comfortable casting around two ounces.

The system is showing signs of being outdated by modern specimen rods, which can be pushed a lot further than their test curve readings might suggest.

There's some very good, budget priced rods for the budding specimen hunter. Carbon composite, 11 foot models can be purchased for between £35 and £50.

Slimmer full carbon blanks from 11 to 13 feet - the extra length is desirable for long range casting - cost between £70 and £300.

KEY PERFORMANCE FEATURES

A: The open-faced fixed spool – first choice for any newcomer.

B: Wide line roller which rotates smoothly is vital.

C: Stern drag with variable settings is adjusted to release line if the pressure exceeds the breaking strain. The anti-reverse switch is turned on to prevent the reel backwinding.

Some fixed spool models have automatic bail arms. They work on a trip mechanism, so if you flick any part of the bail with your index finger as you cast, it will open in one movement and release line. These reels are popular with competition anglers where speed is so vital.

Most fixed spool reels have manual bails. This isn't a handicap as it doesn't take long to get used to opening the bail with your free hand, before casting. Then the index, or second finger of the rod hand is used to trap line against the spool as the rod is positioned. The line is released and allowed to flow out freely as the rod is brought forward to cast the tackle.

Some fixed spool designs have front drags, or clutches, but on the majority they're mounted at the rear. One slight advantage of the rear drag is that it doesn't get in the way if you need to make any adjustments while playing a fish.

The function of a drag is to regulate how line is released from the reel when the bail arm is closed. Some anglers set the drag lightly, as an added insurance if they strike a bit hard. This should prevent the hook length from breaking and also guards against line breakages when playing a good fish, should it bolt off unexpectedly.

Some experienced anglers prefer to tighten the drag right down, relying solely on backwinding the reel if a big fish runs hard with the tackle,

but it's safer to slowly work up to this stage.

Another important feature to look for on this particular reel design is the line roller. This is located to one side of the bail arm and on a good reel will rotate as line is retrieved. It protects the line from excessive wear as you wind in heavy tackle, or a fish, and it will also cut down on line twist and generally gives your reel line a longer life span.

Many reels now have ball bearing actions. One ball bearing is usually good enough to make a reel very smooth in its handling. Top models may have two, or three and this does make a noticeable difference, producing even greater

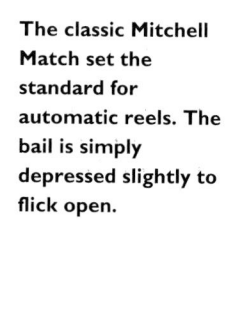

The classic Mitchell Match set the standard for automatic reels. The bail is simply depressed slightly to flick open.

**Front drag fixed
spool.**

**Shallow match spool
and deeper model for
heavier lines.**

Bottom right: **Closed
face reel - copes well
in a facing wind.**

smoothness, which in turn helps to eliminate problems when bringing in fish and tackle.

Most reels have two options for engaging the bail arm. The first and most often used is automatic. Simply turn the handle and the bail springs back into place and you can start start retrieving line.

The alternative is manual. The bail is folded back into position with your free hand and clicks into place. This is preferable when trotting your tackle on running water.

If you strike and connect with a fish while the bail is open, you will have already trapped the line against its spool with one of your rod hand fingers. Now your free hand can close the bail onto the line. This prevents any slack line, or jolting movements, which might result in the hook losing its hold.

Any attempt to transfer a taut line from its trapped position by winding the bail arm shut, causes all sorts of problems.

When viewing reels you will notice some have shallow and others deep spools. Many models in fact come with two, or three spools and these may vary in depth.

Shallow spools are for lighter, float fishing

reel lines in the 2 lb to 3 lb breaking strain category. Deep spools take thicker, stronger monofilaments and are either for legering, or heavier duty work.

It's also worthwhile remembering that wider designs of line spools tend to store the line better. It won't twist-up so easily and certainly shouldn't tend to bed-in, which can cause casting difficulties.

CLOSED FACE Closed face reels, as the name suggests, have a housing over the line spool. There's also no bail arm. Instead, the line is released by pushing a button, or skirting at the front of the reel.

These models are very popular on running water. This is because the line can be very tightly controlled as it is fed out. This helps when trying to slow float tackle down, against the flow, which is often a vital way of enticing bites on hard fished waters.

The closed face has a pick-up pin hidden inside. This will retract as the front button is pushed to release line. The pin will then re-engage as the handle is turned, so once a fish is on, the line can be easily wound off your fingers – if a fish has been hooked while trotting the tackle.

Closed face reels are mainly used for short range fishing, but most match anglers also carry them as a back-up for awkward conditions, where a facing wind might cause problems with fixed spool designs.

These models will cope with longer casts, such as when fishing waggler tackle, but often a slightly bigger float with a heavier loading is required to get the required distance. The enclosed line is restricted slightly when casting with these reels.

CENTREPIN Centrepins are not recommended for beginners. These are specialist reels, and take some getting used to, mainly because they are so free running and need operating in a very controlled manner.

Although centrepins can be used in diverse ways, they have gained a reputation as excellent trotting reels. This is due to the way the reel will rotate on its own – if the tackle is balanced correctly – when fishing flowing water. This method relies on top and bottom attached floats. By gently prodding the drum of the pin, as the tackle is laid onto the water, the drum will carry on rotating and feeding line. This results in a unique form of tackle presentation, keeping the float leaning back as it trots.

In plain English, it causes a very slight slowing down of the tackle and this technique is particularly favoured by anglers after river roach – a species renowned as fickle feeders.

The other main role for centrepins is for fishing close-in when after another river species, barbel. This type of reel can be used when laying on with float tackle, or when fishing a light link leger. Barbel tend to bolt when they pick up a bait and sometimes conventional reels can't cope with this initial surge.

But the centrepin has no restrictions on the line and responds well to these sudden demands. Some models do have drag settings, but these are very light and will still release line fast enough to compensate for an unexpectedly sharp pull. In

Specialist centrepin built by Dave Swallow of Ringwood has milled edge on the drum for improved grip.

fact, the clicking sound the drag makes is often used by barbel specialists as a bite indicator.

HOW THE POLE SCORES

While rod and line fishing is an essential part of learning the art of watercraft, there is another equally effective way of catching fish and that is with the pole.

Earlier this century, the roach pole as it was known, was something of a specialist item, limited to just a very small band of canal anglers. In those days poles were heavy, being made from bamboo, or other hollow woods. But because they were longer than most rods, advantages were exploited in catching shy biting fish like canal roach.

A shorter line between the pole tip and float

REEL POSITION TILTS BALANCE

It is very important to position a reel correctly on a rod. Many beginners fix the reel too far down the handle, making the rod feel top heavy.

In 99 per cent of cases, it's best to fit the reel very close to the top of the rod handle. This achieves a balanced position and the rod won't feel over-weighty if you are holding it for long periods.

It also means you can support the butt of the handle under your elbow when playing a good fish, so the increased weight puts less of a strain on your arm.

Check that the reel fittings fit flush to the corks and offer a secure hold for the reel without any suggestion of slackness or wobble.

Fit the reel in this position and you'll achieve a better balance.

The great benefit of a pole is its ability to present ultra fine tackle with absolute precision.

results in more bites being hit. That's especially true with baits like hempseed, which bring lots of very fast bites.

The roach pole re-emerged as a good catching method with the advent of fibre glass models, but these were still relatively heavy and cumbersome. Pole fishing only really began to be taken seriously with the emergence of carbon fibre models.

The method also soon lost the 'roach' tag, because the new breed of extra long and extremely light poles suddenly opened new doors, as a very potent way of catching most species on most types of venues.

Today's poles are very sophisticated. Top of the range models extend as long as 15-16 metres. Most ten-metre models are also very manageable in one hand. Space age technology has advanced incredibly the strength, lightness and stiffness factors in carbon poles.

The main disadvantage with pole fishing used to be the lack of give, if a big fish was hooked. Anglers had to rely on the finer tip section to absorb punishment on the end tackle. The tip was often referred to as a flick tip and these are still used for some types of pole fishing, particularly when after small fish.

Often, this wasn't enough to stop good sized fish and pole anglers resorted to ringing up poles, even fitting them with small reels.

The main advancement in pole fishing, has been seen in the internal shock absorbing systems now being used. Much of the development in this department originated in this country, even though it was the Continentals who actu-

ally started the pole revival several years back.

Specially treated pole elastics come in numerous grades, specifically designed for different species and sizes of fish.

There's also special PTFE bushes which are fitted at the forward end of hollow top sections of the pole – through which the elastic emerges. This self lubricating material keeps everything smooth running.

But the main secret of pole fishing undoubtedly lies in superior presentation of tackle and hook baits. Often, when the running line angler is struggling to present his tackle in an acceptable manner, the pole man is capitalising. Much smaller and delicate floats can be fished than with running line rigs.

This translates into better, more hittable bites. The tackle can be manipulated to encourage bites when the fish aren't really in a feeding mood. It's possible to edge the hook bait along the bottom, to lift it invitingly, sometimes to virtually coax it into the fish's mouth!

The pole will also hold a hook bait dead still when the water is racing through – a feat near impossible with rod and reel tackle. Long poles can also be used to lower baits into areas not very accessible to rod and reel.

An experienced pole man will not be afraid to drop stepped-up tackle into a tiny opening in thick weedy areas, or guide his float right up against the opposite bank cover on canals, or small rivers. The long pole will often extract particularly good fish from such areas, simply because the pole tip is directly overhead and it can be used to steer the fish from snags. There is noticeably less control with the shorter rods.

The distance between the pole tip and float is also minimal compared to running line, so even shy, half hearted bites are hittable.

BUYING POINTERS

When shopping for important items of tackle, make sure that the product feels right. Don't be swayed by sales talk. If an item seems comfortable in your hands, remember it will be you who will be using the rod, reel, or pole at the end of the day!

Tackle choice is difficult for a beginner, so it's better to try and lead the retailer into showing you several items in a particular category. Then you can choose, rather than being directed to one product.

It's uncanny how a rod, reel, or pole which feels right the first time you pick it up, turns out to be exactly that when you get it on the bank.

There are many other pointers here which will eventually become second nature as experience grows.

When picking up a rod in a tackle shop, ask the tackle dealer if he would mind pulling the tip down. This indicates the rod's action and what it will handle. (It is better to let the retailer do this anyway because accidents do happen and it's more likely to be at the tip end of a rod, rather than the handle!)

If you're also purchasing a reel, don't be afraid to ask if you can fit one to the rod you like. It needs to balance and you won't know this until you try.

When holding a fully assembled rod you also want to try jiggling it about a bit. This trick soon exposes any loose joints. Normally you will hear them knocking, you may even feel this transmit up the blank. Don't be afraid to request another rod from the stockroom, if there are any doubts.

When selecting a reel, make sure it sits securely on the rod of your choice. If it's loose, ask the tackle dealer if he can change the reel grips on the rod. Plastic ones are superior to alloy and might only add about £1 or so to the bill!

Also, make sure you can reach the front edge of the line spool on a reel with the fingers of your rod hand. This is very important, so you can feed out line, or cast properly.

Look for free running reels, not stiff actioned ones. If the bail arm engages jerkily, look to another model.

Check before you commit yourself to see if a particular model is supplied with spare spools. If it doesn't, make sure that the extra spools are easy to obtain.

Pole choice is the most difficult of all. You can ask to be shown the pole outside the shop if it isn't big enough for the pole to be fully erected. Remember most long poles feel good at 8-10 metres, but some suddenly turn very sloppy in action as 11, or 12 metre sections are added. Insist on seeing the whole pole erected!

Also make sure the sections fit properly and will come apart with ease. You don't want to spend the next six months constantly rubbing male sections down with wet and dry to get a good fit!

A very good tip when a pole is fully set up is to ask someone to hold it, while you take a look back down its length from the tip end. It's amazing how this will highlight any badly sagging sections. A good actioned pole will have a very gradual curve. Steer clear of models with butt section sag. This tends to transmit down the whole length, when you strike and generally adds up to a sloppy action.

Another important question needs asking here – is the pole supplied with any spare tip sections? These will inevitably be required, so you can carry several grades of elastic shock absorber, ready set-up. Ask about the availability of spare sections, just in case you need any more, or suffer an accidental breakage. Most tackle shops offer a good after sales service.

A ROD FOR EVERY JOB

Venue choice and the angler's objectives generally influence tackle selection. So an angler who intends to exclusively fish big rivers may be happy to go equipped with a tip actioned float rod and maybe a medium to long range feeder rod-as a back-up. But this gear wouldn't suit a canal, or lake venue. A softer, through-actioned float rod would be more suitable here and for legering, or feeder fishing, softer quivertips are required to spot what are often more leisurely and less positive stillwater bites.

The angler concentrating on canal fisheries might well select a pole as his first line of attack while those with big fish in mind will want stiffer actioned specimen rods.

All this needs to be borne in mind when visiting a tackle shop. State your objectives as precisely as possible and the tackle dealer should be able to pinpoint your exact needs.

ACCESSORIES

There are hundreds of accessories in coarse fishing from bread punches to waders. Here is a small selection of the more important items which will almost certainly become part of your kit.

BAIT WAITER

The idea of the waiter is to keep the bait conveniently close to hand. Regular feeding is made a lot easier if you don't have to stretch for hookbaits and groundbait.

The most common type is made from moulded plastic with recesses to take standard bait boxes. There's a centrally fixed screw with a standard thread which fits most bank sticks. It's a good idea to use an adjustable stick to position the waiter at the right height, for both sitting and standing.

Table top waiters are popular with competition anglers and the most versatile are fitted with four adjustable legs making them suitable for hard banks like canal towpaths. This particular design holds up to six square bait boxes.

The most basic waiter is a simple aluminium tray with a bank stick screw fitting.

CARRYALL

Most standard carryalls feature a side pocket with drainage holes for the keepnet and landing net. The main compartment is for bait boxes and there's usually enough room left for a flask.

Deluxe carryalls may have extra end pockets for accessories like catapults and bags of groundbait. These usually have a zip-up top flap, so the contents are kept dry.

The better carryalls are fitted with a shoulder strap, as well as the usual carrying handles – useful for long hikes to distant swims.

BANK STICKS

Most anglers carry a selection of bank sticks in various lengths and thicknesses – larger diameter ones are usually more robust.

The most versatile bank sticks are telescopic, either those with a locking nut, or perhaps a thumbscrew, so they can be fixed at exactly the correct height for whatever accessory they are supporting.

All bank sticks have a uniform thread, so they will accept just about any rod rest head, keepnet, angle lock, target board, pole roller, or bait waiter.

Bank sticks are usually made from a lightweight alloy, but practically all of the more expensive and durable designs are made of stainless steel. Most bank sticks have pointed ends, but you can get some flanged types. It is worth remembering, however, that the flanged ones won't swivel round in soft ground.

KEEPNET

Basic keepnet shapes are round and square. Round nets are generally cheaper and surprisingly often have a longer life-span. Square nets store neatly in carryalls and offer the fish more room if you tend to visit venues with very shallow margins.

The main drawback with square designs is that the corners tend to wear out quite quickly. But you can purchase special clip-on edge protectors which will prolong the life of the net by preventing the corners from rubbing against rough bottoms through wave action.

It's best to buy a large net if only to be fair on the fish you intend to keep in it. Longer nets are handy anyway when fishing from awkward high banks, or in shallow margins so you can stake the end sections out into deeper water.

Net materials vary in mesh sizes and some are fitted with a sacking type base which provides a dark sanctuary for the catch. Knotless keepnets which are soft to the touch have become universally used following bye-law changes which have created minimum standards for the whole country.

Mono mesh, which is quick drying and odourless, has also become popular and is equally kind on the catch.

Always stake keepnets out and, if possible try to position them in a shady area. You shouldn't aim to retain fish unless you really have to and then don't keep them in nets for over-long periods.

FLOAT TUBES

While it is possible to store many floats in tackle boxes, some have awkward shapes, or are too long. It's possible to buy round or square float tubes. Some also have the handy facility of extending for protecting those really long wagglers. If you haven't enough room to keep a tube in your tackle box or carryall, it's often possible to slip one in a side pocket of a rod holdall. Some anglers use float tubes to store spare quiver and swingtips.

ROD HOLDALLS

The best holdalls feature a padded shoulder strap, plenty of room inside the main compartment for protective rod tubes and a couple of side compartments for umbrella and bank sticks.

Some holdalls open from the top and a zip runs at least a third of the way down their side for easy access. There are also roll-up versions which open out completely.

In the tackle shop you'll see some designs which accept up to ten tubes, standard models take about five or six rods, but there are specialist, longer holdalls which are used by carp anglers in particular. These have side reel pockets so two piece specimen rods can be strapped inside with the tackle made up.

Check the strength of the stitching because the holdall is almost certainly going to be subjected to a great deal of wear and tear. Drain holes in the base and umbrella compartment are also desirable.

The average holdall should last for many seasons so make sure your choice of model meets all of your requirements.

ELECTRONIC BITE INDICATOR

Electronic bite indicators with audible alarms and visual LED displays are chiefly used used by carp and other specialist anglers, especially when fishing with more than one rod.

The top-of-the-range indicators usually have volume and tone controls and a latching light which comes on for several seconds, directing you to the right rod.

CONTINENTAL TACKLE BOXES

Expensive continental tackle boxes are constructed with lift-up trays, or pull-out drawers, which usually comprise the top section of the box.

The lower section holds larger items such as reels and on many models you'll also discover built-in adjustable legs. The box invariably has a cushioned seat and the leg facility helps you to achieve a comfortable sitting position, even on fairly awkward banks, which is vital when pole fishing.

Systems like the Conti-Box pictured have many optional extras and will almost build into a complete fishing station. It's possible to purchase different size drawer and tray units, to customise the box for your own requirements.

Side drawers allow easy access to small items like hooks, line and shot without having to move from your fishing position.

The base unit holds a surprising amount of gear.

LEGERING REST

For quivertipping work it's advisable to use a wide front rod rest head, with several channels where the rod can be positioned. The Drennan Quiver Rest is adjustable and low slung for easy location. It allows the rod to be critically positioned to gain the optimum setting for the very sensitive quivertip.

FRONT AND REAR ROD REST HEADS

Rod rest heads for float fishing need a wide gape, so the rod can be positioned easily. The front rests should have a groove to prevent the reel line being trapped under the rod, and the back rests must be reasonably deep and stay upright under the weight of the rod.

Some rests are fixed in one position, while others are adjustable with a ratchet, or locking nut system. This facility is very handy on front rests, which are often set at an angle on a long bank stick to position the rod out over the water.

UMBRELLA

The main sizes are 45 and 50 inch. A 45 inch umbrella could be classed as standard size and there's certainly enough room underneath to keep angler and gear dry. The 50 inch models offer more room when the brolly is used to support a bivvy for longer sessions.

Most up-market umbrellas incorporate a tilt device and this is very useful when there's a side wind, combined with rain.

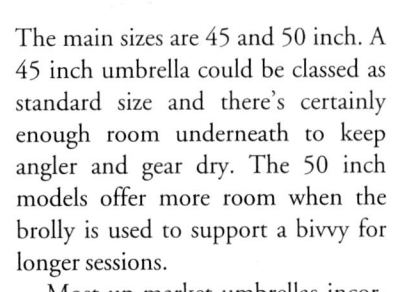

LANDING NET

Round, or pan landing net heads are the most universal. The best types have fine mesh bottoms and larger mesh sides. This prevents them from getting too waterlogged and heavy to lift on a long handle. Rigid frames are preferred to triangular nets with a flimsy front cord.

Triangular shaped nets are favoured by many big fish anglers. These offer a wider gape at the leading edge but, all things considered, I believe that the circular frames tend to be more efficient.

It is possible to use cheaper, alloy handles on smaller nets. But the best handles are of the two or three-piece telescopic glass fibre, or carbon types. Some of these can reach up to ten feet in length, fully extended, thereby reaching over nearside weed. Long, one-piece handles up to six feet in length are popular with specimen anglers.

WADERS

It's a good idea to always keep a pair of waders in the car. They might not be needed on some venues, but will make life a lot easier when banks have been eroded by boat traffic, or where you need to stand out some way in shallow water, so you can cast freely without snagging dense bankside vegetation.

Most waders withstand at least two or three seasons of hard use but leaving the tops permanently rolled down could cause premature cracking of the rubber in time.

Suspend them by the belt straps in the garage when not required – and take great care in the vicinty of barbed wire! That's ruined many a fishing trip and brand new waders.

Wader repair kits are obtainable through tackle shops and adequately deal with small rips.

Never leave waders in the boot of the car between trips – perspiration quickly affects the linings!

TROLLEY PLATFORM

There are some very good angling trollies, which will take tackle box, carryall and sometimes the rod holdall as well.

Other trollies convert into platforms and the Boss Tackle Developments design is a classic example. This model even has pneumatic tyres, to make it much easier to pull large loads over the roughest of terrains.

In its platform mode, this design has six adjustable legs, making it very stable. But it is the greater mobility over uneven terrain that is its greatest strength when compared to those makes fitted with solid, nylon wheels.

There are many venues where it's not possible to get a comfortable sitting position. A fishing platform solves this and also often allows you to gain vital extra yards, by setting up your stall well out in shallow margins.

DISGORGERS

These are essential if a fish swallows the hook. Providing you locate the disgorger's groove on a taut line, and then run it into the fish's mouth, it's a simple task to gently nudge, or turn the hook free.

Micro disgorgers are designed for small hooks and won't damage fine lines. Standard sizes remove spade end hooks from size 14s to 20s. Larger models are suited to most larger spade end hooks and they also work on medium to small sized eyed hooks.

With larger mouthed fish, it's sometimes more practical to remove the hook with surgical forceps.

Brightly coloured disgorgers which float are probably the best buy, as these tend to disappear from the tackle box with frustrating regularity.

Alternatively, use a lanyard attachment to suspend the disgorger from around your neck or keep it propped in the bait box.

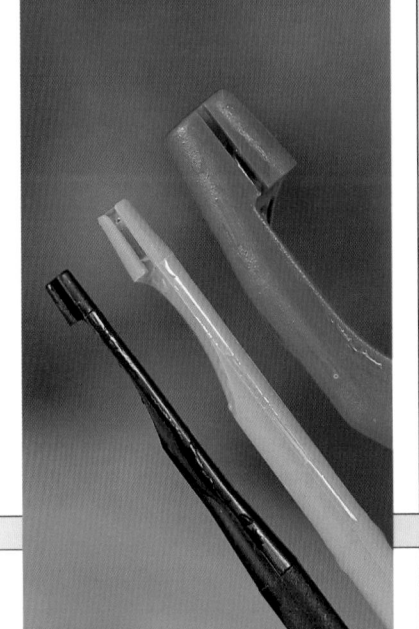

SCALES

Clock face scales are easy to read and usually incorporate an adjuster for zeroing in the weigh bag. Lightweight, compact sets can be stored away in a tackle box just in case you want to check-out the weight of an exceptional fish, or catch. There's also very expensive and highly accurate match fishing scales which weigh down to grams and can cost several hundred pounds.

Spring balances are even more compact and surprisingly accurate. These are not sophisticated enough for serious competitions, but are fine for personal use. Tubular versions like the Salter are available in several weight bands.

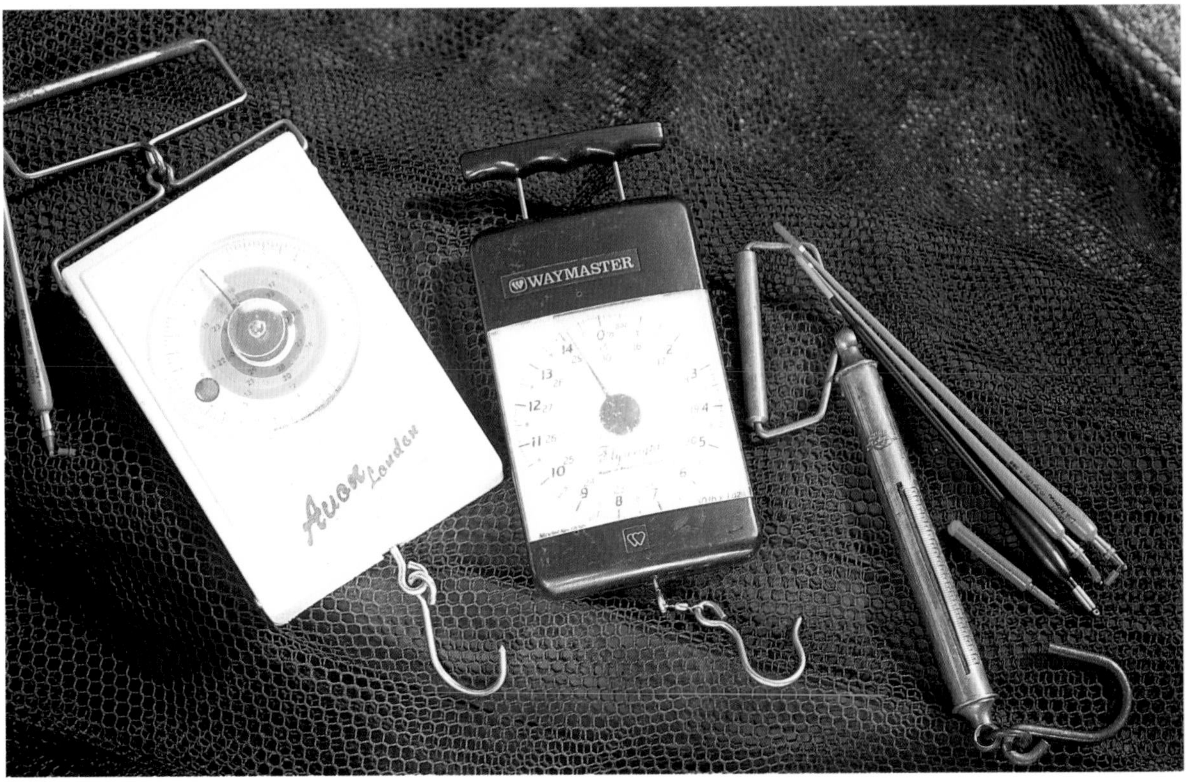

Shot Pliers

Non-toxic shot is rather too hard to bite onto the line. A pair of shot pliers allow you to position the shot perfectly, apply just the right amount of pressure and fix the weights exactly where you want them.

Shot pliers can also be used to move stubborn weights which might otherwise damage fine lines. Loosen the shot by applying pressure against the split. This should open the shot's grip enough to be able to slide it to a new position.

Other Gear

Chairs

While most coarse anglers choose to sit on solid tackle boxes, some prefer the comfort of lightweight chairs.

The Shakespeare design folds away neatly and has a carrying strap. Fox designs have adjustable legs for use on uneven banks and are low slung, making them comfortable for extended stays at the waterside.

These are by far the most versatile and feature disks on the feet to stop the chair sinking into soft mud.

Groundbait Mixing Bowl

Although you'll see square mixing bowls in the tackle shop, round models are more practical for achieving really consistent ground-bait mixes. By adding water gradually and stirring vigorously, the water is worked into the whole mix. With square designs it's possible to miss groundbait which collects in the corners. Clean out the bowl after the session to avoid the build-up of stale fragments.

Target Board

In summer and autumn, bites are mostly easy to spot when quiver or swingtipping. But this changes in winter when the fish are more lethargic and may only move the 'tip a fraction of an inch. By positioning a target board, as a backdrop behind the bite indicator, these very small indications are magnified.

A target board could make all the difference on really dour days.

ALL ABOUT BAITS

Opposite: **Segregate your baits in spacious boxes to keep them as fresh as possible.**

Good, fresh bait catches the most fish. Watch any expert angler setting up by the waterside and you'll see different baits, such as casters, maggots and hemp, all carefully segregated in their own bait boxes. If the weather's hot, and the angler has travelled some distance to the venue, he may even have transported the bait in a cool box.

It is worth seeking out local tackle shops which have a reputation for selling quality bait. Those shops which are popular with matchmen will usually stock the biggest and freshest maggots and casters.

Buy your maggots neat and check that the bran, maize meal, or sawdust is added after they have been measured out into your bait boxes. Beware of tackle dealers who only dabble in fishing gear. They may not have good refrigeration facilities on the premises and offer you a pint containing old, small maggots and dirty sawdust. You'll end up paying the same price for a poor product and much less of it!

Good bait draws more fish into your swim. It also behaves in the correct manner to catch fish. Old casters and sweaty maggots often float, which are no good if they drift out of the swim. Fresh bait also hooks well. It is softer skinned and more attractive to the fish.

TIPS ON STORAGE AND PREPARATION

Right: **Riddle out any sawdust or bran before starting to fish.**

Bait quickly deteriorates if it's not looked after correctly. Maggots, casters and cooked hempseed should be stored in a fridge, particularly if they're collected well in advance of an trip.

Clearly, it's not always practical to keep livebaits in the kitchen. Keen anglers solve the problem by purchasing a cheap, second-hand fridge for use in the garage.

If you don't have this facility, there's still a lot you can do to maintain bait in a reasonable state. In hot weather, place your casters and cooked hemp in a cool box, along with a couple of ice packs. You'll need to replace the ice packs every 12 hours.

Out of a fridge, maggots are best stored in lots of sawdust, or bran. It is important to give them plenty of air to keep them cool. This is best achieved by laying them out in large, shallow trays. Position them in a shady, dry place, such as a shed, or garage floor.

Casters are purchased in plastic bags, normally in either pint, or half pint measures. If they're to be retained for any length of time, casters require air to keep them alive and prevent scorching of their skins against the bag. They will use up what little oxygen is inside, so it's best to open bagged casters after eight to 12 hours and to breathe them for five minutes. Also shake them in the bag, so those pressed up against the sides get moved.

You'll need to reseal casters to retard their development because if they are allowed to darken too much they become floaters. But when sealing a bag of casters, it's prudent to leave a little air inside.

Maggots stored in a fridge should be kept in open topped, deep sided containers. Sawdust and bran are the best storage mediums. Maize flour helps keep maggots soft, but don't put too much of this on the bait while it's stored, because it cakes-up and may make the maggots damp. Maize is, in fact, best added to maggots just before you go fishing. It revives and softens flagging bait, absorbs any excess moisture and makes the bait easier to riddle and feed.

Most anglers carry a small maggot riddle in their kit and shake off any storage media on the

Hemp and casters – a winning combination.

Right: **Sometimes a specific colour of maggot like bronze works better.**

bank, before starting fishing. Neat bait is easier to feed and you don't get a face full of sawdust every time you throw, or catapult some maggots into the swim.

Hempseed is a very good attractor and holds fish well. It can work on its own, but is also very potent when used with maggots and casters.

It is easy to boil your own hemp in an old saucepan. Remember hemp swells to almost double its original volume, so you need to carefully gauge how much you think you will need. Pour the dry seeds into the saucepan and add approximately the same amount of water. Bring this to the boil and then let the bait simmer, until most of the seeds slightly split open and are showing small, white shoots.

When the bait reaches this stage you will need to wash it off with cold water –this is best done through a strainer –in order to stop it from over-cooking. Cooked hemp can be stored in the freezer compartment of a fridge. It's not a bad idea to prepare and bag up a large quantity all at once, so you can take a pint or so as it is required.

If the hemp is still frozen solid by the time you reach the venue, it will thaw out in just a few minutes if you drop a bag of it in your keepnet and suspend it in the water, while you tackle up. If you are short of time and facilities, cooked hemp is available in most good tackle shops.

COLOUR AND SEASONAL FACTORS

Many pleasure anglers are happy to go fishing with a pint of maggots and perhaps a small bag of groundbait. This simple approach catches fish, but often a little research before an outing can make you better prepared for the particular way a venue is fishing.

The types of baits which anglers regularly feed

REVIVING STALE BAIT

In an ideal world it would be nice to take perfect bait on every trip, but things go wrong! The tackle shop might have the odd late delivery, or coldroom problems in really hot, humid weather. Large volumes of maggots are very hard to keep. They give off a great deal of ammonia, which is a constant worry to the tackle dealer. The ammonia eats through pipework, causing a big cold-room to lose gas and unexpectedly heat up. So very occasionally you are bound to get some slightly below par bait, no matter how good your supplier.

There may also be the odd occasion when maggots sweat-up on the way home from the bait shop, or you simply forget to transfer them to the fridge. Whatever the reason for livebait getting out of sorts, it will result in some shrink-age and give off a rather nasty odour.

Warm, active bait deteriorates fur-ther if you take no action. It's best to quickly riddle it, which is the fastest way of cooling it down and this process also removes smelly sawdust. Add clean dust, or bran which will clean and cool the maggots further.

Poor bait can also be revitalised by adding some concentrated flavouring. There are specially formulated maggot flavourings you can buy in the tackle shop, and liquid flavours used by carp anglers on boilie baits are also suitable. Sweet and savory smelling baits will enhance your chances of catching. A good flavouring will also help to draw fish to maggot baits in coloured water more quickly.

Add some flavouring to revitalise stale bait.

into different venues strongly influence what the fish will accept. In many cases, they will become preoccupied with a particular type of bait and you could be wasting your time by trying to wean them onto something else. There will, of course, be occasions when a different approach works wonders but in general it's advisable to follow form.

There are few venues where you won't get bites on maggots. This is, after all, the best selling bait up and down the country. But you'll find a particular colour works better on some waters, bearing in mind commercial maggots are widely available in white, bronze, red, yellow, fluorescent pink and sometimes even an exotic green!

The fish might prefer a specific colour because it is used most frequently by anglers or closely resembles their natural food. In either case, if you have done your homework, you are likely to experience more action if you have the right shade of maggots.

In similar fashion, a water may respond better to casters than maggots. This is often the case when after bigger fish. They might have grown wary of maggots, or the casters could mimic a natural food on which the fish like to forage.

Another point worth remembering with an inert bait like the caster, is that it won't attract smaller fish as readily as a lively maggot. Putting a caster on the hook might take you longer to get a bite, but it also gives bigger, slightly less active fish a chance to find it.

Bait requirements change with the seasons. Some are more associated with summer fishing. A classic example is sweetcorn which is productive for species like tench, bream and carp, from June right through to September. But once the first signs of night frost appear, it rapidly loses its effectiveness.

Although hemp attracts fish and holds them in a swim for most of the year, as a hookbait it only fishes consistently in the warmer months. This applies to most seed baits.

Other baits have good winter reputations. When the water is really chilled and goes very clear, it can be a devil of a job to buy a bite with maggots, and yet a small piece of worm, jigged along the bottom, will entice an immediate response.

Small pellets of bread, known as punched bread, fished with a cloudy groundbait will also bring a lack-lustre swim to life.

Matchmen often turn to baits like bloodworm and jokers in winter. These are the bottom dwelling larvae of the midge and represent the

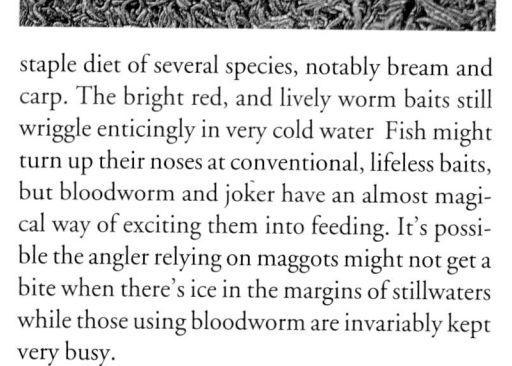

Above: **Punched bread – capable of bringing a swim to life when fished with cloudy groundbait.**

Left: **Bloodworm – wriggle enticingly in cold water.**

staple diet of several species, notably bream and carp. The bright red, and lively worm baits still wriggle enticingly in very cold water Fish might turn up their noses at conventional, lifeless baits, but bloodworm and joker have an almost magical way of exciting them into feeding. It's possible the angler relying on maggots might not get a bite when there's ice in the margins of stillwaters while those using bloodworm are invariably kept very busy.

HOW MUCH BAIT TO TAKE?

The best policy is to try and take a selection of baits with you on every trip. Obviously, if you've discovered a bait with good form for the water in question, this will be the No.1 line of attack and form the bulk of what you take. But if you also carry smaller quantities of other baits, you have other options if bites dry up at some stage.

It's also a good idea to feed different baits in different parts of the swim. That allows you to rest an area, and this is a ploy which very often brings the first line back to life again, later on in the session.

THE ROLE OF GROUNDBAIT

Groundbait has to be tied in closely with feed baits and, of course, hookbaits. The type of groundbait you use is also dictated by venue characteristics and the target species.

There are many different types of groundbaits, but selection is made easier, if you bear in mind the most important reasons for using it. These are:

■. To attract fish.

■ To act as a carrier to get other feed baits into the swim.

■ To hold fish in the vicinity of the hookbait.

Groundbaits can be mixed in differing ways, regulated by the amounts of water you add. That way it's possible to achieve different consistencies. You can also purchase different consistencies. Some are soft, fine and cloudy. There's also very heavy, binding mixes...and quite a few in-between! It's also perfectly viable to blend several mixes together, in your search for a special consistency.

Cloudy groundbaits are normally used in stillwaters. Regular feeding of them tends to spur fish into activity on hard waters. This type of mix also pulls fish up, off the bottom.

There's lots of medium consistency groundbaits. Most Continental brands will form a cloud if mixed very dry or wet, but mix them somewhere in-between and small balls of feed begin to disperse as they near the bottom. This type of groundbait is the most popular, because it's ideal for feeding squatts, bloodworm, jokers and casters.

Heavy, binding groundbaits are used to stiffen softer mixes. On their own they make a good carrier for getting loose baits to the bottom in flowing water. They will form larger balls, which break down slowly after they reach the bottom of a swim, releasing particles of other baits which have been mixed in.

Small amounts of some heavier consistency groundbait are also used to pack the particle baits into open-end swimfeeders.

It is possible to form plugs of groundbait at each end of the feeder trapping the particles inside.

Taking the right quantity of bait is often determined by the type of venue and the species you are after. Normally, you'll need more bait on a river, or when seeking big fish like barbel. Generally, on flowing water you'll need to feed not only more heavily but also more regularly, to draw and hold the fish otherwise they'll drift away in the current.

Lake fishing is often more leisurely, unless you know very big catches of bream, tench, or carp are on the cards. For a normal lake session, you might get away with half the quantity of bait considered essential for a river.

Canal requirements are usually for very small amounts of more varied baits.

Excluding groundbait, a realistic bait menu for a river session could be two pints of hemp, four pints of bronze maggots and a pint of casters. The hemp would be loose fed on the float line, along with maggots, or casters. If this didn't work, there would still be enough maggots to consider a change to the swimfeeder – a method which can use up several pints of maggots over a few hours' fishing.

On a lake outing an angler might take one pint of hemp, two pints of casters, one pint of red maggots, half a pint of red and fluorescent coloured pinkies and perhaps a small pot of red worms.

There's much less quantity here, but still plenty of options. Casters and hemp could be fed on a running float line and red maggots can work well on the hook with this combination. If the swim didn't respond, the pole could be tried with the red maggots, or if the fishing was really hard, the smaller pinkies might come into play. A third option might be to try the open-end feeder with a mixture of hemp, caster and pinkies as feed. In this case, the casters and pinkies are candidates as hookers with worm and red maggots possibly worth trying.

Canal fishing might demand a pint of white squatts, half pint measures of casters, hemp and mixed pinkies, a small pot of worms and maybe just a handful of some larger maggots to try on the hook.

There are countless pole methods that could be coupled with this small but varied amount of bait. The waggler, or even a light leger rig might also be used at some stage.

All these examples are by no means hard and fast ones. They demonstrate how bait quantities and types should tie in with the type of venue and relevant methods. There are also plenty of good back-up baits, which you won't necessarily need to obtain from the tackle shop. Many anglers get in the habit of slipping a few slices of fresh white bread into their tackle boxes. This provides some useful bait options on many types of venue.

A tin of luncheon meat might sit in your tackle box for several outings, but sooner or later it could catch you a big chub, carp or barbel.

Sweetcorn is another bait that can swing things your way – especially when small fish are mopping up maggots rather too avidly.

CHIEF HOOKBAITS AND THEIR USES

MAGGOTS Standard big maggots in their natural form are an off-white colour. They're sold in various dyed shades of bronze, red, fluorescent and yellow.

White maggots are pretty universal in their attracting qualities and catch most freshwater fish. Bronzed are next in popularity and make particularly good river baits for species like chub, roach and barbel.

Red is a colour which has great appeal to lake species like tench, bream and carp. Red maggots also score well in highly coloured water and are a good all-round bait for perch.

Fluorescent dyed maggots usually turn out as very bright, mixed shades of oranges, pinks and reds. These are good change baits and their high visibility is an advantage when legering, or float-fishing off the bottom.

Yellow maggots are also a good change bait. They retain high visibility when fished in really deep water and have a reputation as superb roach and dace baits.

Maggots are best hooked through the small flap of skin at the tail or blunt end. This procedure won't burst them and makes them still wriggle enticingly.

Pinkies are about one-third of the size of big maggots. They have been given their name because of their pink tinge in their natural form. They can be purchased dyed bronze, red and fluorescent pink.

This small maggot is very effective on harder canal fisheries, both as feed and mounted on tiny fine wire hooks. Pinkies are often fed in groundbait mixes, especially in the open-end feeder. Red and fluorescent types are good for skimmer bream and perch. White and bronzed ones are popular for roach, skimmers, dace and gudgeon.

Squatts were originally only used in groundbait, as a holding feed, by bream anglers. These tiny maggots are only half the size of a pinkie and the advantage of feeding them in groundbait is that they remain static when immersed in water. Fish easily pick them off the bottom, but won't tend to be over-fed by them.

Over recent years the squatt has also evolved into a top match fishing bait on canal venues. It can still be fed in groundbait as previously, but other very successful pole and waggler techniques involve cupping and catapulting this bait

out neat for small and medium sized fish.

Maggots eventually turn into chrysalids or casters and if you catch these at an early stage of development they make a superb big fish bait. In their very early stages, they are white, then they turn pale orange. Left open to the air, casters keep on darkening, progressing to a lovely bronze colour and later to a reddish, dark brown. Finally, they turn almost black.

From their white form to their early brown state, casters sink in water. The lighter they are, the quicker they sink. The darker they become the slower their fall rate. Normally, a bag of casters contains a mixture of colours and their differing fall rates in water often prove very attractive to fish.

Most anglers prefer casters when they are orange, or bronze. Canal anglers might let their bait progress to slightly darker stages for harder venues, but this must be carefully regulated, because if they mature too much they'll float!

Floaters only have minimal applications. They can be useful as feed on some well stocked carp lakes, when the angler wants to get the fish boiling on the surface. A floater used as hookbait sometimes fools very wary fish, as it disguises the weight of the hook.

It takes several pints of maggots to get a few good pints of casters, so most anglers purchase them from the tackle shop. These normally have to be ordered a few days in advance as this is a very popular bait.

Casters have a big fish reputation for most species and are equally effective on lakes, rivers and canals. They are excellent to use as feed because they lay lightly on the bottom and won't bury into silt, weed and gravel like maggots.

Casters can be lightly hooked like a maggot, but their other advantage is you can completely bury a hook inside them, which is a great way of enticing big fish in clear water.

WORMS Several types of earthworms are widely used in angling. The largest are lobworms which have excellent fish drawing qualities, especially if chopped up and introduced into the swim neat, or in groundbait. These are also used whole, or in sections, on large hooks for big fish like chub, carp and barbel.

Brandlings are the most common worm you'll find on sale in tackle shops. This is because they're relatively easy to produce. Brandlings are an effective bait for many species, particularly bream, perch, chub and roach.

Redworms are harder to source, but if you can

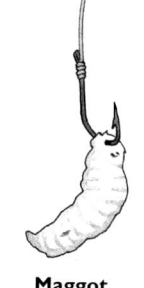

Maggot

Lightly-hooked maggots (through blunt end) will wriggle enticingly.

Caster

Caster (hook buried)

Hook casters in similar fashion to maggots when fish are feeding freely.
Bury the hook inside to fool wary big fish.

Whole lobworms are great attractors for many species including greedy bream.

Worm

Hook small worms through the head segment for best presentation.

obtain a supply, they make superb bream, perch, chub and roach baits.

All worm types, including the common earthworm, can be chopped up and used in groundbait. Another more recent winning method, particularly when the going is hard, has been developed by pole anglers. They fit a special cup on the end of their poles and carefully tip neat chopped worms over the float line. This often brings a quick response from perch and also works for skimmer bream, tench and carp.

Bloodworms and their smaller, livelier cousins, jokers, are collected from the bed of streams and lakes. This is hard work, particularly in winter, so these baits are expensive. They are also very effective when sport nosedives in cold weather. Competition anglers are the most likely to consider these expensive baits viable. They also tend to pull lots of smaller fish, useful to the match angler, but not perhaps everyone's idea of what fishing should be about.

SEEDS Hempseed has an attractive smell when freshly cooked. It also produces an oily residue, which roach in particular seem to find very attractive. As a feed, hemp is a good attractor in most venues and for a cross section of species.

As a hookbait, hemp mainly scores in the summer and autumn months. It performs best in clear water for roach, but will also tempt chub, hybrids and dace. This is a specialist bait, which requires very regular feeding in small amounts. It produces lightning fast bites, mostly on-the-drop, and tackle must be spot-on.

Tares are cooked in a similar fashion to hemp but are a much larger, more filling seed. They're softer and can be used as a hookbait with hemp. Tares often produce more positive bites and apart from catching 'hemp' fish like roach and chub, also give better chances of connecting with other species including carp, barbel and bream.

Sweetcorn can be fished over hemp. But it's also a bait with good drawing powers in its own right. This is mainly a summer bait, associated with fish like tench, bream and carp. It attracts big fish, so sturdy tackle is in order.

BREAD, MEATS AND CHEESES Bread is an amazingly versatile bait. It works in flake, crust and paste forms. It can also be punched out into compressed pellets on a flat board, so it stays more firmly embedded on smaller hooks.

Fish with a preference for bread baits are tench, bream, carp, roach, chub and barbel. It's a cheap, worthwhile option on many venues.

Luncheon and sausage meats are renowned big fish baits. They can be fished with other baits and feed, but also suit the roving approach and will often bring savage takes almost immediately, if dropped into fishy looking swims with cover. These baits are excellent for chub, barbel and carp.

River anglers have recently been experimenting with raw steak and minced beef and taking big catches of chub. This method originated on the River Trent, but is spreading fast and gains a response on float and feeder methods. Strips of steak are used on the hook, while mince is mixed with groundbait as an attractor.

Most cheeses can be formed into a paste, if need be, kneading them into a bread base. The stronger smelling ones are favourite for chub and barbel, if large pieces are shaped around big hooks. Smaller pellets of cheese paste will take roach and bream.

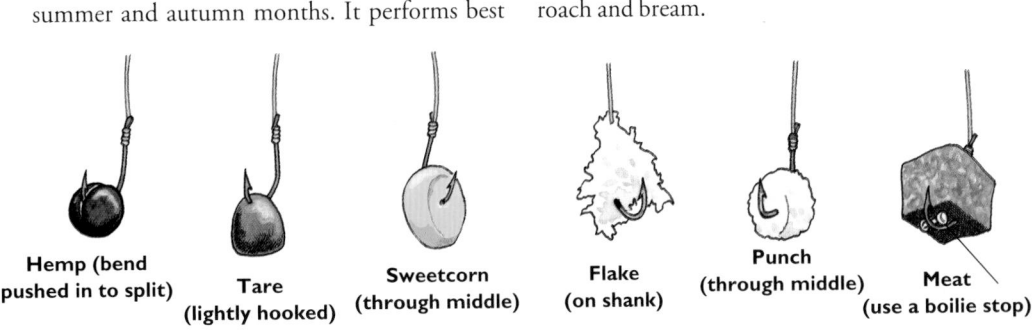

Hemp (bend pushed in to split)

Tare (lightly hooked)

Sweetcorn (through middle)

Flake (on shank)

Punch (through middle)

Meat (use a boilie stop)

BOILIES Ready-made boilies have advanced over the years from frozen baits into more convenient shelf-life packs. They're now bagged and sealed in a phenomenally wide range of colours and flavours, and in four diameters: micro, small, medium and large. Neutral boilies which need dousing in the flavour of your choice are also obtainable.

These little balls of high protein are sold with savory, seafood and fruit based labellings. There are many exotic recipes and if these don't take your fancy, it's possible to buy basic ingredients and produce your own concoctions.

It's difficult to make boilies work on waters where they've never been used, but where they are regularly introduced, the fish are soon weaned over to them. In fact, on many carp lakes the fish are preoccupied on these rich baits and the name of the game is finding out which type and colour are most in-vogue.

This information is normally gleaned from the local tackle shop, or the bailiff. It's also a good idea to pick slightly different, but related recipes, if the water is heavily fished.

Boilies are primarily directed at carp, but bream and tench also become dependent on them where lots are fed.

The beauty of these baits is that they're usually immune to the attentions of small fish and single out the specimens instead.

Hair-rigged boilie pivoted from mid-shank with a short length of silicone.

GROUNDBAIT TACTICS

On some occasions, loose feeding alone provides a good day's fishing. But there are many other times when groundbait brings far better results. Sometimes a delicate balance of the two methods is needed.

It's very difficult to explain how these decisions are made because even the most experienced anglers get it wrong! Mainly, it's a case of feeling your way. When there are other anglers about, it's wise to loose feed carefully at the start and check to see if those using groundbait are getting results.

The response you get from loose feed, often directs you towards using groundbait anyway. Sometimes you get the feeling loose feed is bringing too slow a response, or failing to hold fish. But it's certainly a better idea to start any session carefully and gently build up your feeding regime. That's definitely preferable to throwing mounds of stuff at the fish. Once feed is deposited in the swim you can't get it back!

If you do decide to kick off a session with groundbait, it should be done carefully. It can always be stepped-up later. Try a couple of experimental balls of groundbait and if they bring no results, little harm will be done. You can then revert to loose feed.

Sometimes you might find the fish in a strange mood as they respond initially to loose feed and then fade away. You try groundbait and the same thing happens. In this instance, it's sometimes productive to rotate both methods, feeding groundbait to get the fish into catching range, then reverting to loose feed to hold them...for as long as the bites last. Often this process needs repeating again and again. Groundbait will normally work particularly well when there are many fish about, or on vast waters where a positive approach is necessary to gain a response. There are also methods, like bread punch which rely on groundbait's attracting qualities.

Fish are inquisitive creatures and the splash of large balls of groundbait sometimes lures them in to have a look. There's many a time when match anglers try stirring a shoal into action by bombarding an unproductive swim with several large balls of feed!

As you become more experienced you will undoubtedly reach the stage where you have several groundbaiting techniques up your sleeve. As long as you use these tactically, rather than habit-

ACCESSORIES

A maggot riddle is a worthwhile investment. Apart from running bait through it to remove unwanted skins and other debris, it is also used to produce your own casters – if you want to save bait which is turning.

Groundbait should also be sieved through a maggot riddle, both in dry and mixed form, to ensure it has a better consistency.

There are also smaller meshed pinkie and squatt riddles for running small maggot baits and for the important job of cleaning off sawdust and sand.

In the tackle shop you'll see a good selection of round, square and sometimes even partitioned bait boxes. Some are now even escape proof!

Make sure you buy a bait box for maggots that's plenty big enough. This bait needs air otherwise it will sweat-up. Square boxes store particularly well in carryalls.

Some shops sell shallow hooker boxes for small baits like bloodworm. These are insulated to keep the contents cool in summer and prevent freez-

Square bait boxes store neatly in carryalls.

ing in winter. They usually have a flip-top which avoids wind drying the bait out. Most have a screw fitting at the base which allows the box to be positioned nicely to hand on a bank stick.

If you intend to use bread, a punch board gives a firm base to compress the bread, so it stays on the hook better.

Most of the commercially manufactured boards have an outside lip and double up as open topped hooker boxes.

A selection of plastic bags are always handy for storing a variety of baits. Casters store well in these, as do hemp, tares and dry groundbait. Some anglers carry a couple of extra bags in their kit and may save unused groundbait at the end of a session. This will last several days in a fridge if it's sealed properly.

ually, groundbait will often make a big difference to your catches.

MIXES

The most basic groundbaits are brown and white bread crumbs, sold in varying grades from fine to coarse. There's also a special type of coarser, punch crumb. This is white, but is freeze dried, so it won't bind together like normal white feed.

Brown crumb produces a good cloud mix while white in its natural form is a good binder. Punch crumb fragments on hitting the water to give a very attractive trail of mixed size particles as they descend to the bottom.

White is mixed with brown crumb to achieve different consistencies. A minority of anglers swear by pure bread feeds and they do work well on numerous venues.

But many anglers find bread feed on its own too bland for their requirements. Apart from offering many different consistencies, Conti-

nental groundbait mixes also give amazing colour and flavour options. You can still bulk these out with basic bread feeds, but the resultant mix has a far more potent aroma.

Many rich ingredients go into Continental feeds. Some are obvious like crushed hempseed, maize, biscuit and powdered sweetcorn. These additives are thought not only to hold the fish for longer but also to attract certain species, more than others.

In this area, Continental groundbait specialists such as the Belgians, Dutch and French are arguably more advanced than ourselves. They are very keen on specialised recipes, aimed at particular types of fish and venues. In fact, many ingredients which go into their most popular groundbaits are kept secret.

That is why much of the Continental groundbaits that you'll see on the shelves in tackle shops are clearly labelled for specific venues and species.

It's certainly worth experimenting with them,

Add water sparingly to crumb and Continental groundbait mixes – and not the other way around.

perhaps together with bread feeds, because they do achieve consistent results.

Because Continental mixes are more expensive than plain bread feeds, it's a good idea to bulk them out with crumb, particularly when a fair amount of groundbait is required. This makes them go further and also achieves a slightly more manageable consistency when the feed is wetted.

In winter, when less groundbait tends to be used, it's much better to introduce Continental feeds neat, as it really utilises their superior drawing powers.

Always mix water, in small amounts, to your groundbait, not the other way around. By adding water gradually and stirring vigorously with your hands, you'll get a nice, evenly dampened, fine consistency. Try pouring dry groundbait into water and it goes very lumpy! It's also hard to regulate the correct amount of moisture this way.

Most anglers wet their groundbait just sufficiently to get a dry, fluffy mix, then leave it for five minutes. This allows it to absorb the moisture properly, then the process is repeated two or three times, until the mix feels and looks right.

Neat Continental mixes are sometimes harder to work because they may be less absorbent. Give these their first application of water the night before you go fishing, so they have plenty of time to fully absorb and expand. Then, any finishing touches can be applied on the bank.

Probably the best mixing bowls for groundbaits are the round collapsible type. These store neatly and help achieve more even mixes. Square bowls are passable, but it's difficult to get at the dry groundbait which collects in the corners.

Collapsible, round groundbait bowl – makes for a good mix.

FIRING AND FIXINGS

A: Three essential catapult designs – Image canal caster, Canal King mini model and a groundbait cradle.

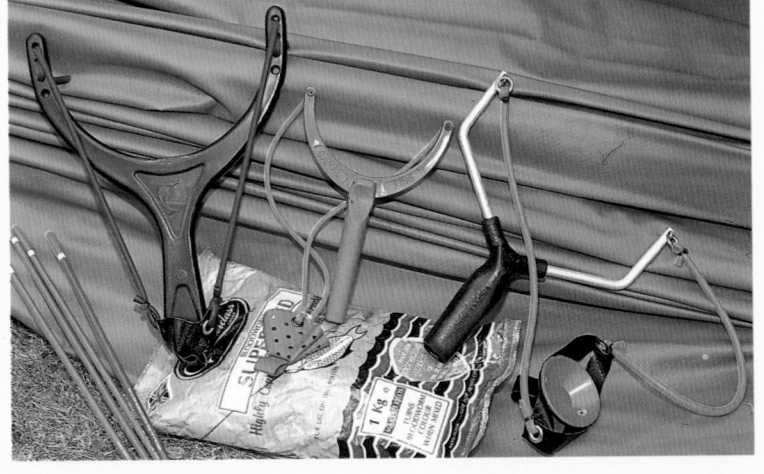

B: Great ingenuity has been shown in fixing catapult elastics to the frames including the use of a split ring and electrical tie.

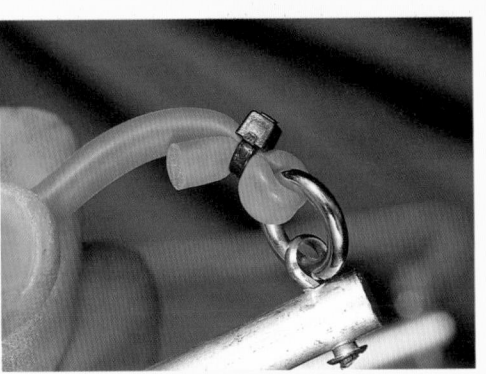

C: Threaded latex fixing developed by Image.

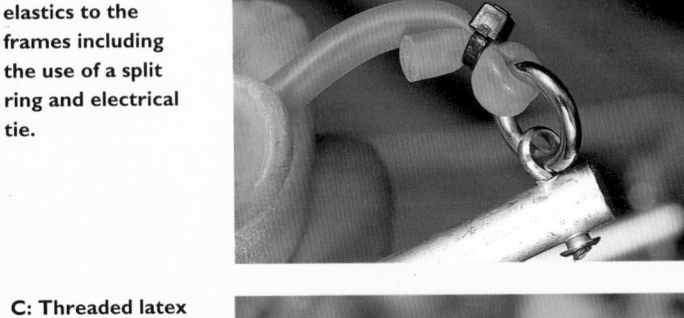

D: Plug and push-fit attachment.

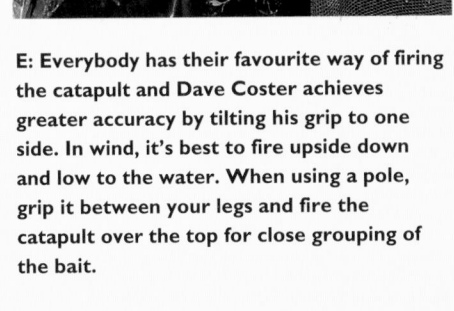

E: Everybody has their favourite way of firing the catapult and Dave Coster achieves greater accuracy by tilting his grip to one side. In wind, it's best to fire upside down and low to the water. When using a pole, grip it between your legs and fire the catapult over the top for close grouping of the bait.

CATAPULTS, CUPS AND DROPPERS

Loose feed and groundbait have limited scope if fed by hand, but there are some excellent purpose designed catapults for both methods. Loose feed catapults tend to group the bait better and certainly give far greater distance than is possible by throwing it in. Groundbait catapults extend your feeding range up to 80–90 metres and they are very accurate.

The pole cup is a useful device on hard canal venues. This gadget clips on the tip section of the pole and is manoeuvred out precisely over your fishing area. Small quantities of neat baits, or groundbait are then tipped into the swim inch perfectly. This is better than risking the odd, misplaced helping of feed, which might ruin your swim completely.

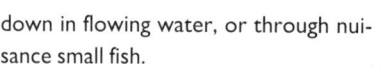

Bait dropper in action

Bait droppers are fixed to the hook and lowered, or cast into the swim with your tackle or a spare rod rigged up for the purpose. They have quick release mechanisms which open a side, or base flap as they hit the bottom. This results in loose feed like maggots, or casters being deposited in a very tight area. Bait droppers work well in getting feed down in flowing water, or through nuisance small fish.

Throwing sticks are another way of loose feeding in a reasonably tight circle, slightly beyond arm range, with maggots, casters and hemp. There's also specialised boilie throwing sticks, which will put these baits out quite accurately up to 70 metres.

Above: **Pole cup tips bait exactly where you need it.**

Right: **Boilie throwing stick.**

Below: **ZLT mini and Thamesly droppers.**

Right: Spade and eyed hooks.

HOOK CHOICES

There are countless hook designs in every conceivable shape and colour. Each pattern might have several uses and as many as a dozen sizes. Some series run in even numbers – 16, 18 and 20 are popular sizes – while certain specialised match hooks graduate in odd sizes, such as 17, 19 and 21. High numbers are designated to small hooks, while smaller numbers signify larger hook sizes. The largest freshwater hook is a size 2 and they go as tiny as size 28s or even minute 30s for match fishing purposes. Many are chemically sharpened, which in plain terms means their points are finished by etching them in acid. This process produces more precise, longer and sharper points.

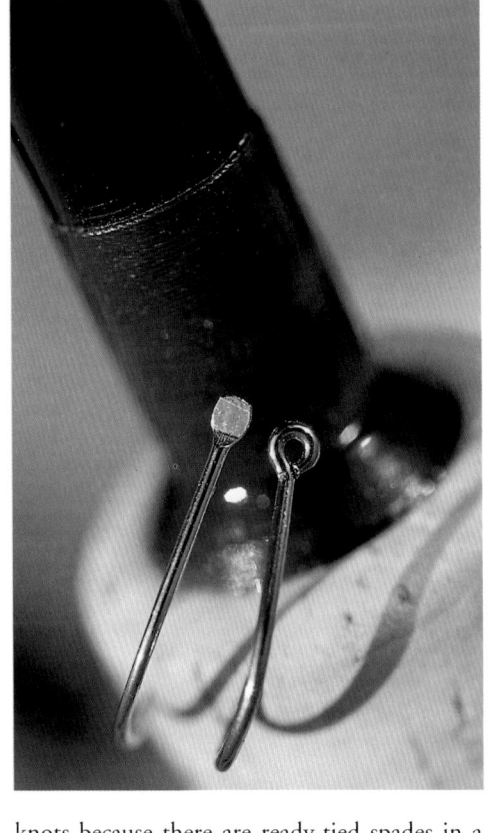

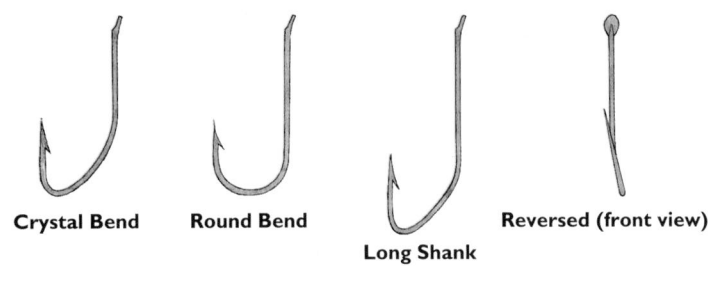

Crystal Bend **Round Bend** **Long Shank** **Reversed (front view)**

Some hooks have large barbs, but modern patterns are more conservation minded and possess micro, or whisker barbs. There are also barbless patterns which are easiest to remove.

Anglers tend to classify hooks into two categories – eyed and spade-end. Eyed hooks are formed with a small ring at the top of their shanks through which the line is threaded, making them the easiest to tie. Spade-ends have a flattened flange at the top of the shank which the knot butts against. Sophisticated knots are essential here and they may not be within everyone's grasp.

If you can master the art of tying spade-end hooks, it is well worth the effort. These patterns are more streamlined and less obtrusive, particularly in smaller sizes. There's also a far greater choice of designs available to the angler who can master tying a good spade-end knot.

But don't despair if you are all-thumbs at

Right: **Correctly tied spade with the line coming from the inside of the shank.**

knots because there are ready-tied spades in a variety of patterns and nylon strengths. Manufacturers are now producing the right kind of relationship between breaking strains, hook designs and sizes. Some products are nearly as good as top anglers might achieve, but shop carefully, because there are also a minority of inferior, poorly tied items.

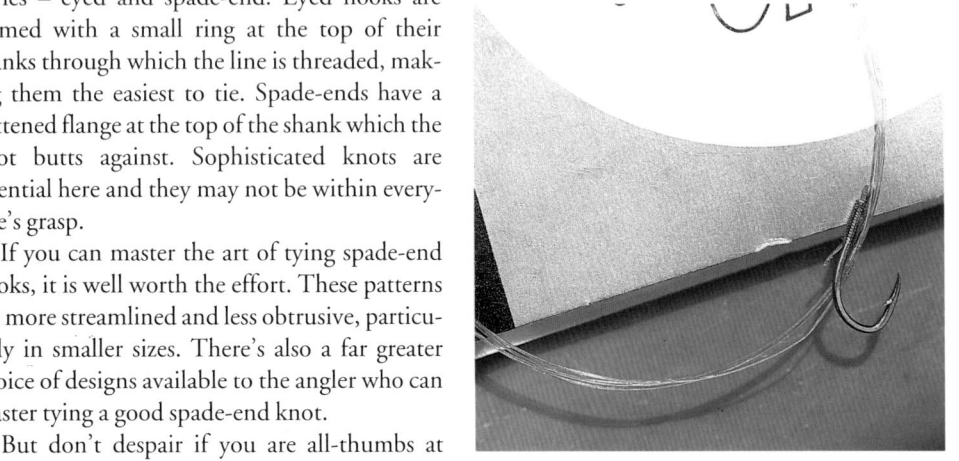

COLOURS, SHAPES AND WIRE GAUGES

The majority of hooks are finished in bronze, gilt or silver colours. But colour coatings, which give red, green and blue finishes have become increasingly popular. Therefore it is now possible to select a hook pattern to tie in with most bait colours.

For example, pale silver hooks are popular with white baits like bread punch and squatts. Bronze hooks obviously suit bronzed maggots.

Red hooks are identical in hue to bloodworms and are hardly noticeable when attached to red maggots. Gilt, or gold coloured hooks match sweetcorn and yellow maggots. Dark blue hooks make a good choice for casters and hemp.

Hook shapes, or patterns are also selected to help present certain baits better. Crystal bend hooks are widely considered superior for maggots, mainly because these lively baits can't wriggle free from the steep bend which precedes the upward turn to the point.

Round bend patterns tend to have slightly wider gapes and are very good for seed and bread baits.

Reversed, or offset hooks have points which slightly lean to one side, rather than pointing directly upwards. These offer increased hooking potential on feeder and leger tackle.

Long shanked designs make hooking small baits like bloodworm a much easier task. Sometimes, short shanked patterns produce more bites from wary canal fish.

Design considerations like these often boil down to personal preference –but the question of wire gauge or thickness is crucial. Fine wire hooks are light and less likely to cause a fish to reject a hookbait. They also help achieve balanced tackle when fishing with fine diameter lines on harder venues.

Obviously, there are limits to the size of fish you can realistically aim for with some light hooks, although expert anglers land some surprisingly big fish on them. If this sounds confusing, the trick is to use as light a hook as you feel safe with.

Medium wire hooks are probably most popular and prove adequate for a lot of general fishing situations.

Forged hooks are very strong, but their extra weight and bulkier appearance might result in fewer bites –unless they're disguised by using a lighter, or buoyant hookbait.

On certain venues like fast flowing rivers, a heavy hook has a negligible effect. Feeder fishing demands this type of hook anyway, especially at long range, where a savage take from a chub, or barbel would straighten out a fine wire design very easily.

In the interests of preserving fish stocks, some fisheries insist on anglers using barbless, or micro barbed hooks which are easier to extract.

Barbless hooks offer advantages. They need less power to drive them home and they are the easiest hook to remove from fish. They are popular for short pole fishing, stick float and light waggler work.

A small barb is preferred when fishing at distance with baits like maggots, because it helps stop them wriggling off the hook. The barb will also ensure baits stay on when legering and helps to keep a good hook-hold on fish when unshipping sections of longer poles.

HOW TO WEIGH UP NYLON DIAMETERS

The numerous brands of nylon line broadly fall into two main groups – reel and hooklength monofilaments. But it's not quite that simple, because some reel, or standard diameter lines, also double as good hooklengths.

There are major differences between standard monos and the so called low diameter lines which offer a much higher breaking strain for the same, given diameter. This combination of low diameter and high strength allows anglers to experiment with much finer hooklengths than with standard monos.

Standard lines have thicker diameters in relation to their breaking strains. Their strength is also often under-stated, so there is a safety element here. They will do more than their labelling suggests. Standard line is also more robust, again due to its thicker diameter.

Low diameter, high tech. lines have been a revelation over recent years. They offer greatly reduced diameters if you equate them against the same breaking strains in standard lines. This gives the angler a much better chance of fooling wary fish. Lighter lines make hookbaits perform more naturally. They are less visible and certainly much more supple when a fish draws the bait inside its mouth. All in all, this adds up to more bites.

KNOT TYERS AND STORAGE SYSTEMS

If you experience difficulties tying spade-end hooks, there are some good hook tyers on the market. It may take a little practice to perfect techniques, but these devices are relatively easy to use and form secure knots.

It is possible to tie hooks on the bank, but make a habit of doing it at home, the night before a session, and it will save valuable fishing time. Fragile hooklengths should be stored carefully, to avoid damage and tangles.

There are several hooklength retaining devices including colour coded plastic spools and fluted plastic boards around which hooks and nylon are wound. Wallets with pouches or plastic, see-through sleeves are another option.

The small, plastic winders used by

Right: **Trace board with pins stores hook lengths neatly.**

Below: **It's possible to store running line rigs on pole winders.**

Reversed spade-end knot

pole anglers to store complete rigs are also useful for hooklengths. Some anglers make up complete running line waggler and stick float rigs and keep these on larger pole winders.

Small chemically sharpened hooks rarely need any attention on the bank. If they blunt it's probably quicker to tie on a new one. Larger hooks lose their points more easily when legering over rough ground. Therefore, it's sensible for you to carry a small hook sharpening stone for these occasions. It will only take a couple of seconds to hone the hook point back into good shape.

The down side of this new technology, lies in the safety factor being lost on low diameter lines. Their breaking strains are spot-on and there's no buffer against mistakes like over zealous striking or attempted bullying of fish into the landing net before they are ready. Being a lot thinner, they are also far more prone to tangles and spinning-

up on the retrieve. In addition, low diameter lines are less hard wearing.

All this leads us to the conclusion that the standard monofilaments are still best for use on the reel. They absorb an incredible amount of wear and tear – which they need to do as they are repeatedly cast and retrieved.

PICK A LINE FOR THE JOB

Some standard lines are more hard wearing than others. Some are more supple or sink well. Others have built in floatability. All these factors suit particular methods such as the waggler, stick float and leger.

For instance, sometimes it's essential to keep the waggler still and if the surface is drifting badly, you will need to cut a sinking line under the water.

Floating lines are essential for top and bottom attached floats like sticks to work the swim properly. A buoyant line mends more easily, without pulling the float off course. It also lifts from the surface swiftly as you strike.

Sinking lines are obviously preferred for legering.

It's advisable to opt for standard lines as hooklengths when a rugged bottom or strenuous long range work, imposes extra stresses on the terminal tackle. These lines are also best when big catches and hefty fish are expected.

Low diameter lines come into their own for hooklengths when seeking small fish or when the fishing is hard. They are also used extensively on the pole as main line and hooklengths, because their thinness greatly improves tackle presentation. These lines don't suffer so much wear on pole tackle, because most anglers use elastic shock absorbers.

It's best to gain some experience before trying low diameter lines as hooklengths on running line rigs. They need special knots and careful treatment when retrieving them and unhooking fish. They also weaken after several good fish have been landed and, as a result, may need changing regularly.

Many anglers now refer to their lines by diameter, rather than breaking strains. Although most spools of line will have both diameter and breaking strain details printed on them, it's a good idea to think this way, because low diameter is a more important factor in fooling the fish.

AVOID UV RAYS

Line should always be stored away from sunlight. Ultra violet light causes monofilaments to deteriorate if they're exposed for long periods.

FILLING THE SPOOL

Before winding new line on the reel, it must be firmly attached to the spool. To the inexperi-

Specialist reel lines. The floating Daiwa brand is suitable for stick floats and the Toray suits wagglers.

Standard workhorse lines – reliable when the terminal tackle is subjected to extra stresses from big fish or snags.

Low diameter lines provide superior presentation.

enced this can be a more difficult task than it appears. You will need to use a slip knot, or arbour knot as it is sometimes known, so the line is pulled tight and grips the reel spool.

And it's critical to wind new line on the reel correctly to avoid it twisting-up badly.

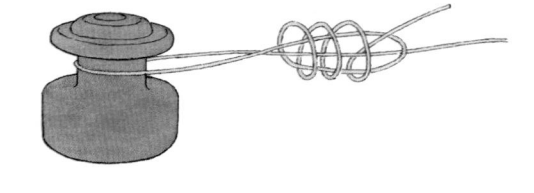

Sliding Arbor knot (three turns are adequate).

Always Use a Lighter Hooklength

Whichever lines you choose, use a hook length with a lighter breaking strain than the main line.

That way, if you're accidentally broken by a good fish, it will not be left trailing yards of tackle.

If your tackle becomes snagged on the bottom or bankside vegetation, a lighter hooklength will break first, again reducing the risk of losing a long length of nylon which could prove lethal to water birds and other creatures.

If at all possible, you should retrieve a lost hooklength from weeds or bankside bushes. It must be cut up into smaller lengths and then taken home and dropped in the dustbin.

Hooklengths rarely need to be longer than 30 inches and in many cases can be made much shorter.

The loop to loop system is the most effective way of joining a lighter breaking strain hooklength to the reel line and it is particularly recommended for low diameter monos. A small loop is formed at the end of the reel line and another at the end of the hooklength. The hook is threaded through the reel line loop and then brought back through its own loop. Finally, gently pull and the two loops will interlock.

Strangulation knots like the tucked Half Blood must be avoided at all costs with low diameter hooklengths because it severely reduces the breaking strain of the rig and its ability to absorb sudden lunges from the fish. The Grinner knot is recommended if you intend using an eyed hook.

Water and blood knots are better suited to joining standard lines. They also significantly weaken the breaking strain of lower diameter lines.

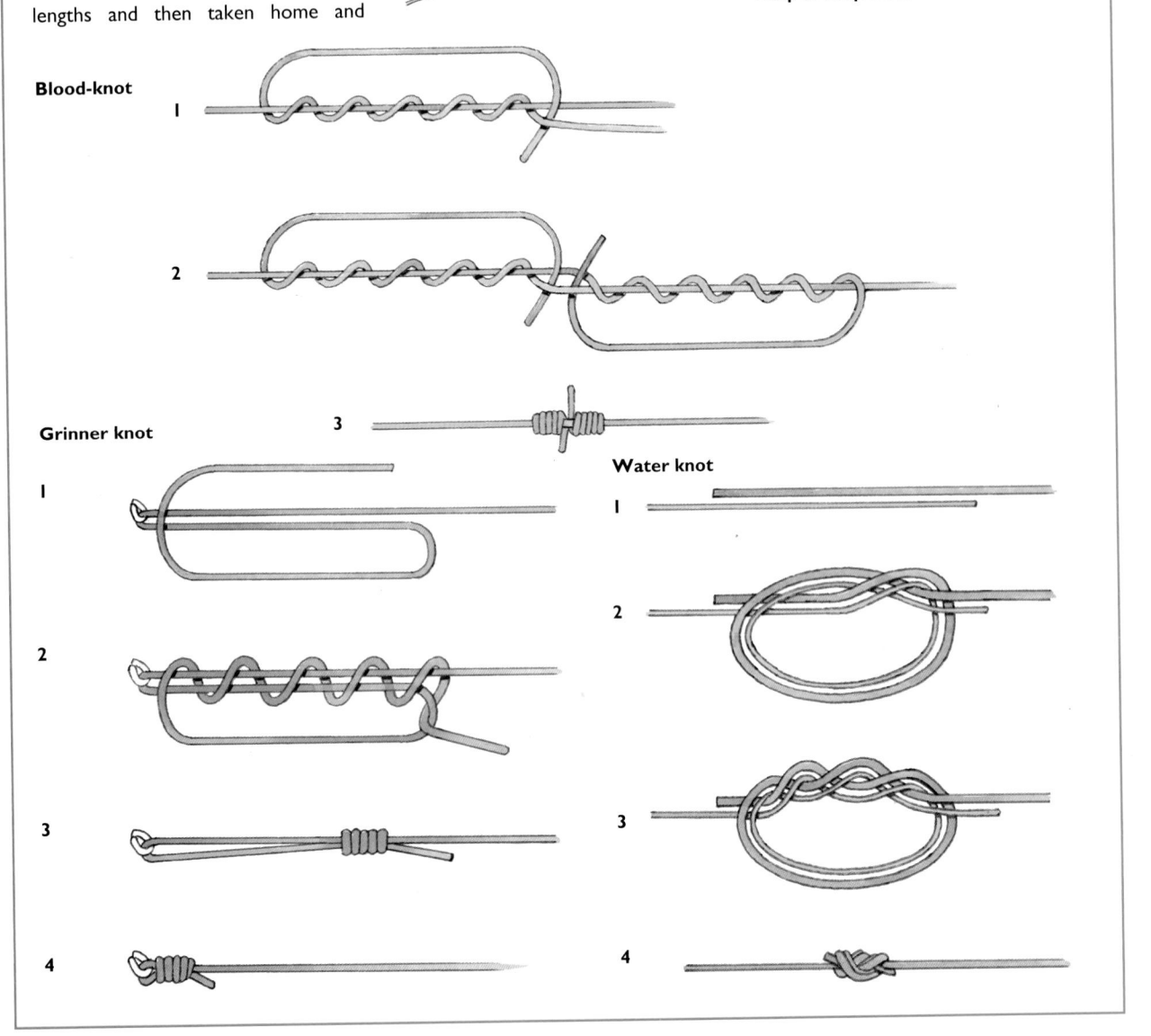

Loop to loop attachment

Blood-knot

1

2

3

Grinner knot

1

2

3

4

Water knot

1

2

3

4

After attaching the line to the spool, mount the reel on a rod and wind the line in through the fingers of the hand supporting the rod. To do this, your rod hand will have to be positioned slightly forward of the reel.

It's possible to regulate how the line goes on the reel in this way, always keeping it slightly tensioned, so it doesn't lie loosely and hinder its flow during casting. Most importantly, you can feel the line as it runs through your fingers. If it's tending to twist, it is leaving the line spool in the wrong direction and the spool will need to be turned over.

Once the line comes off the spool correctly, you will notice the difference. It runs smoothly through your fingers and stays straight.

If you experience problems, ask someone to hold the line spool for you. Get them facing you, so the line is loaded flush to the face of the reel spool for ease of flow. It's best to load reel spools level with the rim. Less line than this will restrict casting distances by creating excessive friction as the line pulls over the spool rim. Over-loaded spools spill too much line off and cause tangles.

SPLIT SHOT

Split shot are non-toxic in sizes larger than No. 8s (0.06 grams). Lead shot are still popular in legal size 8s and smaller as it's considered they present no threat to wildlife.

Leading non-toxic brands include Anchor Double Cut and Thamesly Sure Shot which were among the first companies to develop successful alternatives to lead weights.

Double Cut are less harsh than most alloy shot because of their unique design. They have a normal, 'forward' split which is closed on the line, but also a back cut, which makes the shot more pliable and certainly less severe when applied to finer lines.

These shot are excellent when used as lockers around bottom-end floats. Anchor market two extra and very useful sizes, SAs and ABs. They are also good when formed into strings of bulk shot and as individual droppers.

Thamesly Sure Shot have a black finish and tend to grip the line more firmly than Double Cut which is an advantage on heavier wagglers rigs. Larger Sure Shot can be formed into link legers, and medium sized ones stay firm when strung out, or if they are bulked on fast water float rigs.

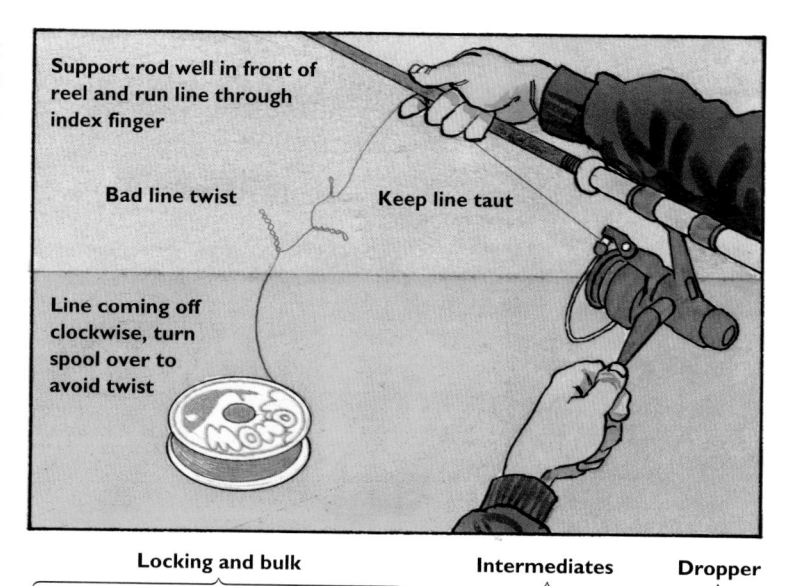

Support rod well in front of reel and run line through index finger

Bad line twist

Keep line taut

Line coming off clockwise, turn spool over to avoid twist

Locking and bulk					Intermediates				Dropper	
SSG	SA	AAA	AB	BB	No1	No4	No5	No6	No8	No10

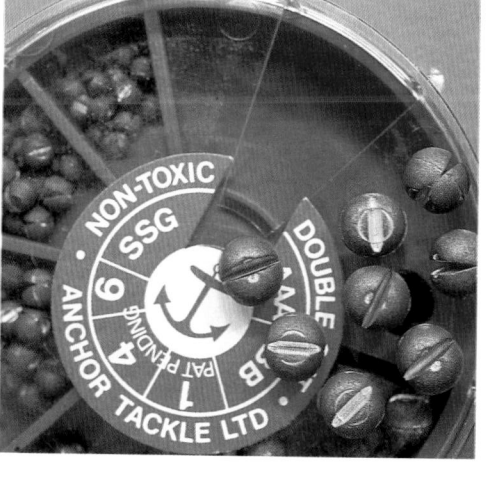

Top: **Loading the reel** If the line is twisting as shown turn the spool over

Above: **Split shot sizes**

Left: **Double Cut shot are kinder on fine lines.**

HOW TO USE DIFFERENT SIZES

Big shot, (SSG, SA, AAA, AB, BB and No.1) are often used to lock waggler style floats on the line. These also form the bulk of the casting weight to

Sure Shot offer benefits on heavier waggler rigs.

STYL WEIGHTS

Styl weights are now available both in lead and non-toxic alloy. They were originally designed for pole anglers, but as running line rigs have become lighter, their use has spread further afield.

Styls are tiny elongated, celery shaped weights, with a groove running down one side. These are very soft, so they won't damage fine hooklengths. Pole anglers use larger Styls spread, or bulked, as their main weighting and

smaller Styls as droppers. They also combine very small dropper Styls with other weights like olivettes and shot.

Because they are soft and sink slowly, Styls are sometimes used as droppers on waggler rigs, for mid-depth and on-the-drop fishing.

Olivettes are used as a bulk weight to speed the bait down to the bottom layers. They're trapped in position with a slender peg or micro shot.

Styls and olivettes.

get the rig out. Larger shot are often called locking shot. They're also grouped to form lower down bulk loadings, when using bigger top and bottom attached floats on powerful rivers.

Medium sized shot, (No. 4, 5 and 6) are usually strung out at equal distances between the float and hooklength, or grouped in a bulk just above the hooklength when fishing top and bottom river floats like sticks, Avons and balsas. They're also utilised as smaller bulks, or as dropper shot down the line on waggler rigs.

Number 8s, or dust shot as they are commonly called, are used for fine tuning rigs. Many anglers taper their shot down in size towards the hook, so the last shot, or tell-tale as it is nicknamed, is a No. 8. This is a vital shot, because it pulls the float tip down to its final setting. This shot won't register on the float if a fish has taken the bait as it settles, and the angler knows to strike.

It's normally very important to keep shot small as they near the hook and not to place them too close. The fish will soon become suspicious if

the last shot is pulling the hookbait down too fast and if it's too heavy, it will cause the tackle to constantly snag on bottom debris. Number 8s are also very good strung out on light stick float rigs, either individually, or in sets of twos and threes.

Shot smaller than 8s are called micro shot. Sizes available are 9, 10, 11, 12, 13 and 14.

There's a call for shots between 9 and 12 as fine tuners, or very small dropper shot on some running line rigs. But micro shot are chiefly popular with pole anglers. They give lots of options in the way small pole floats are weighted.

THE PRIME ROLES FOR A FLOAT

Floats play two important roles. They are bite indicators which is why they've got highly visible, brightly coloured tips. They are also used to present the hookbait in a certain manner at particular depths.

A float only indicates bites clearly and performs sensitively if it is shotted correctly. It's vital to spend some time getting this right, because once a float has been rigged up, you will be using it for long periods. You want it to work for you, not against you.

Many beginners make the mistake of leaving too much float showing above the surface. This causes an imbalance in the tackle and often makes it drift uncontrollably. Worse yet, a biting fish has more float to pull under and might reject the hookbait because of this extra resistance.

Most floats have a fluorescent tip colour and a

Micro shot for fine tuning.

band of white underneath. Shotted correctly, the tip colour alone should be left showing, the white band should be submerged. When a float is dotted down this way, lift bites signal clearly because you will see the band of white rising out of the water.

Similarly, on-the-drop bites also show up well, because the white band won't settle properly and this signals to you that something is going on.

THE MAIN FAMILIES

There's an amazing variety of floats to choose from. Some have specific jobs, others can be classed as all-rounders.

The first important step is to know the difference between river and stillwater float designs. Some cross boundaries here, but there are many types which should be kept to specific usage.

The main families of floats which are fixed to the line top and bottom, such as sticks, Avons, balsas and chubbers, have no valid applications away from running water. These are out and out river floats. In fact, these designs rely on flowing water to work properly. It's important to keep a tight line to them, so the hookbait is trotted on a straight path, or slowed by differing degrees.

If you tighten up the line to these floats they won't go under. A bottom-ender would, so there is nowhere near the same control with other floats on flowing water.

Floats attached to the line by the bottom ring only, known as bottom-enders, or more commonly wagglers, are more versatile in their applications. These are the family of floats to choose when fishing stillwaters, but some designs are also highly effective on rivers.

Wagglers come in straight, stepped, insert, loaded and bodied forms. There are also specialist canal wagglers which are small, streamlined and have very fine tips.

The types of wagglers which most commonly double-up for river fishing are the bodied, straight and insert models. These are very effective on flowing water, at distances beyond those which top and bottom fixed floats are capable of fishing. They may also be used closer in, when awkward weather conditions are spoiling good presentation with top and bottom fixed floats.

As previously mentioned, wagglers won't achieve the same degree of control on rivers, as you can get with out-and-out river floats. But they're effective when the fish are up in the water, or want a trotted bait. Straight wagglers can also be used to drag a bait over-depth. This is the nearest they'll get you to top and bottom float presentation, but clearly it will never be quite as good.

Because our climate is so prone to sudden changes, a fair selection of floats is a good idea. Very often one float of a particular design is not sufficient to cover all eventualities. Floats are usually available in sets of at least four sizes. It's a good idea to buy both lighter and slightly heavier floats, to back-up the particular size you think you'll need. That allows you to step your tackle up or down, should the need arise. You may end up switching to lighter tackle if the fish are shy, or you can add more weight to your rig if a bigger, more stable float is required to combat deteriorating conditions.

STICKS Fishing the stick float is a very prolific way of catching river species like roach, dace, chub and perch. This slim float design is attached to the line with two, or possibly three float bands if you want to prevent slippage in faster water. This method relies on regular feeding, aiming to run the tackle through in unison with the free offerings.

There are different types of sticks. Some have domed tops which work better in faster rivers, others have more pointed tips, which are more sensitive and suit slower flow rates, or fishing up in the water.

Base materials are very important. Light cane will only slowly cock this float –which is ideal

MATERIALS

The materials that go into making floats are very diverse.

They include plastics, wire, glass, quills, reed, different grades of balsa and harder woods. All dramatically affect the way a float performs. Largely it's down to personal preference, regarding the types of materials you lean towards. Some anglers are traditionalists and tend to shun high tech materials like plastic. Instead, they favour natural floats made from quills, reeds and balsa.

That's not to say there's anything wrong with more modern floats. In fact, they often out-perform their rivals. But it's your choice.

Cane, wire, glass and alloy stemmed stick floats, all have their special roles and you will need to be aware of these subtle differences, if you want consistent results.

Popular sticks (from left): mini Gardener, Allerton with shoulder for faster water and Middy. A domed top to the float allows it to be dotted right down for dragging through the swim while a pointed top is more sensitive for holding back. The stepped design is more visible at range.

made from balsa. It's normal to begin a session with the stick, using strung-out No. 4, 6, or 8 shot. These can be regrouped into a bulk, with just a few, or several droppers, if the fish are responding best near the bottom.

BALSAS These are a natural progression up from the stick float, when faster, or deeper water requires more shot to be used. Although similar in shape to sticks, balsa runs right through from tip to base eye. Some balsas are slightly fatter than sticks. The same strung-out, or bulked shotting is utilised with this design, the latter being more popular.

AVONS The traditional Avon has a balsa body fitted to a crow quill stem and tip. There are also versions with cane, balsa and peacock tips. Stems are also made from tapered cane, plastic and straight fibre glass.

Avons are used with large strings of No. 1, or BB bulk shot, which gives them far greater casting range than sticks and balsas and excellent stability. They are one of the best floats to use in very deep river swims.

Far right: **Topper, wire stem and traditional Avons. The balsa bodied Topper is a fine long distance performer while the wire stem works well in turbulent water.**

when fish are taking baits on-the-drop. Heavier canes like lignum give the stick greater casting distance and stabilise it in gusty conditions.

Glass, medium density cane and plastic stemmed sticks tend to be very versatile and take fish at all depths, providing the lower shot are jiggled around to suit. Wire stem versions are certainly the most stable in strong winds and boily surface water.

The top body segment in all stick floats is

Right: **Balsas are the next step up from the stick.**

CHUBBERS These fat, cigar-shaped floats are made from all-balsa, or clear plastic. Their job is to present big baits like bread, meat, lobworms and sweetcorn at long range. They are used with a main bulk, some two to three feet from the

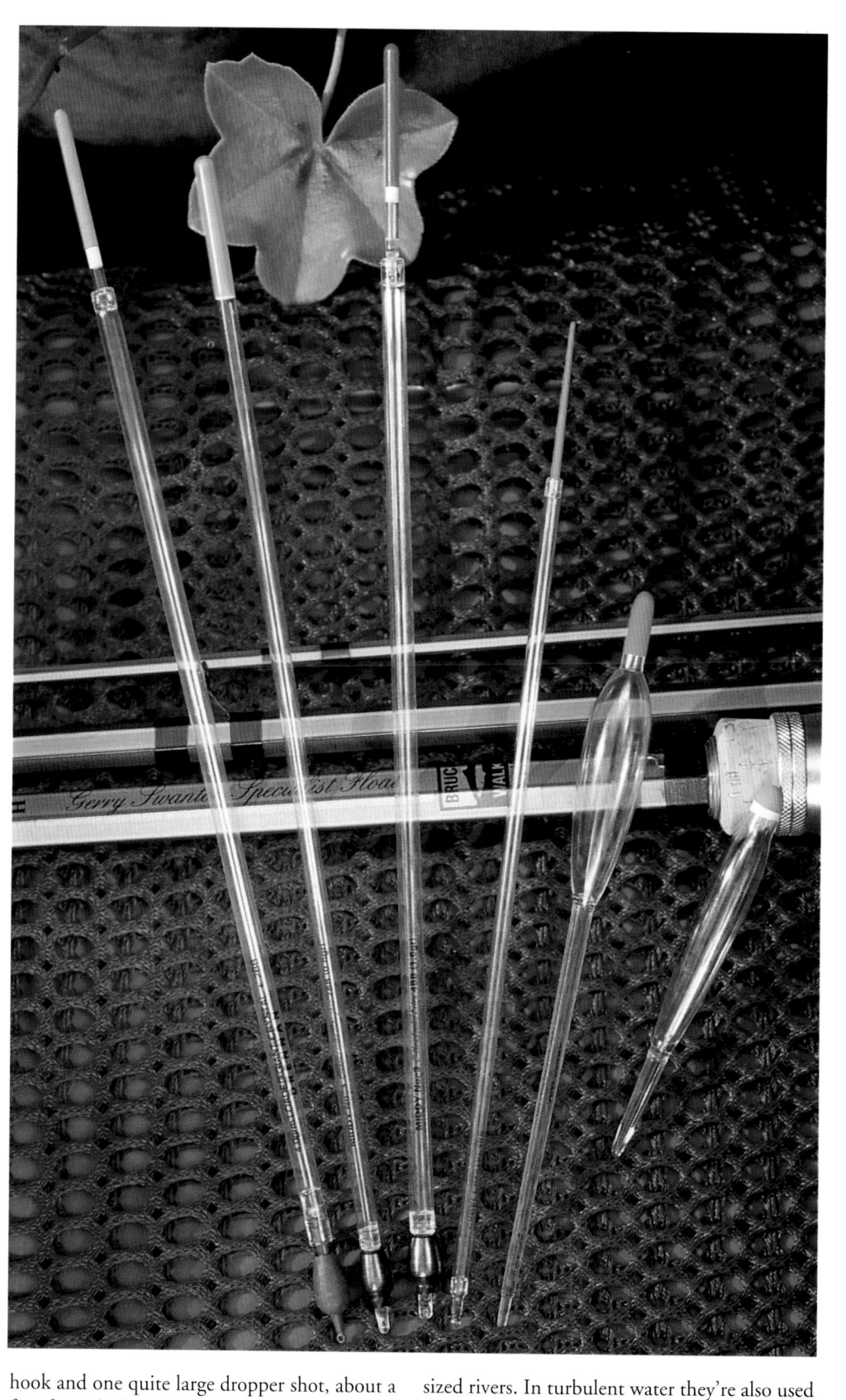

Collection of clear floats including loaded insert and straight wagglers and a fine tipped Canal Crystal. The top and bottom attached floats on the extreme right are Avon and Loafer models.

hook and one quite large dropper shot, about a foot from the hook.

Chubbers cast well and are often used to fish alongside far bank features on small to medium sized rivers. In turbulent water they're also used to present maggot and caster baits. They are good for species like chub, barbel, dace, grayling and big roach.

Right: **Middy C-Thru (left) and Drennan Crystal inter-changeable weighting systems for wagglers.**

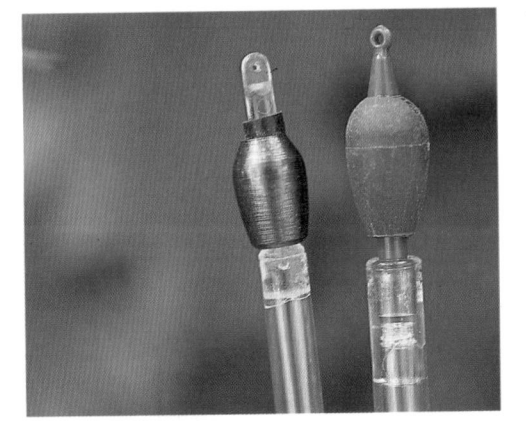

Below: **Loaded, bodied wagglers also function as sliders.**

STRAIGHT WAGGLERS This is the most basic form of waggler. Having a thickish tip, it can be used to fish well over-depth in drifting stillwaters and quite fast flowing rivers. Straights are normally made from peacock quill. Most of the shot capacity goes into locking the float, but in deeper water, more weight can be placed down the line, as long as it doesn't exceed one third of the float's overall capacity. Good for most species.

INSERT WAGGLERS These have a finer tip for greater sensitivity. A good all-round float. They are often used at distance on lakes, or for fishing the far bank on wider canals. Also a good trotting, or up in the water design on slow to medium paced rivers.

Inserts are made from peacock quill, sarkandas reed, balsa, or plastic. Most shot goes around the float, with usually just two or three small droppers spread down the rig. They're good for most species.

LOADED CLEAR WAGGLERS Several companies now produce loaded, clear plastic wagglers. These are available in straight, or insert form. The latter have inter-changable tips which can be an advantage when you are in changing light conditions.

Each design has several float sizes and different weight loadings to match. The loadings can be switched from lighter floats to heavier capacity ones. This can be very handy when slightly larger locking shot, or more dropper shot are required.

Clear loaded wagglers are popular when fishing up in the water, or at range in shallow water. They are less visible in the water and are therefore less likely to spook the fish.

BODIED WAGGLERS An extension of the straight, or insert waggler principle, with a balsa body so more weight can be added for greater casting distances. A very stable float when you find conditions are swamping conventional wagglers closer in.

Some bodied wagglers are made of clear plastic. There are also some specialist jumbo sized ones which are quite often loaded for long range carp fishing.

QUILLS Cut lengths of peacock quill and smaller porcupine quill floats still have a place in angling. These designs are best for close-in fishing, such as laying-on in the margins, or close to weed beds, for tench and bream.

they slide up to and which is usually fixed at full depth. It's best to use bulk shotting with these floats and just one large dropper shot.

CANAL WAGGLERS These miniature wagglers are often shaped entirely from balsa and taper down to very fine, sensitive sight tips. There are squatt and caster versions, the latter have slightly thicker tips for larger baits.

Canal wagglers are also made out of peacock, reed and clear plastic. Generally, these floats are short, so they don't cause a lot of disturbance as they land in shallow water. They are often used bottom-end style on the pole, when drift is a problem, or to-hand style when the water is particularly clear, to keep the pole tip from spooking the fish.

The majority of shotting goes around the float when canal wagglers are used on running line. Smaller shot are used to lock these floats and a bulk used down the rig, when they are used on the pole in deeper water.

ODDBALLS There are quite a few other types of floats including thick, bulbous tipped wagglers. These are called windbeaters. They look strange but in rough water perform rather well, as they don't get swamped by the waves.

Another strange looking float is the Trent trotter, a cut-down bodied waggler. It is excellent when fast river shallows are thwarting your best attempts with conventional stick and waggler floats.

Don't be afraid to make, or experiment with floats which lie outside recognised categories...

Left: **Miniature canal wagglers. There are squatt and caster versions.**

Below: **Quill, Trent trotter and windbeater sight bob.**

SLIDERS Top and bottom sliders are mainly intended for fishing deep stillwaters close in. They also work on slow to medium paced rivers. This design is normally all-balsa, with side and base eyes.

Bottom-end sliders are more commonly used on deep stillwaters and slow paced rivers. They are basically bodied wagglers, with a small loading in the base, to help cock them quickly (so the line can run through them smoothly). They also have a very small base eye, or swivel.

Both types of slider rely on a stop knot, which

PLUMBING UP

Once you have rigged up a float, making sure it's dotted-down correctly so not too much tip is showing, it is time to plumb the swim.

Many anglers hurry this procedure, or approach it in a slap-dash fashion, which is a shame, because it's inevitable they won't be able to take full advantage of their swim.

The most common types of plummets are clip-on and cork based. These will serve you well in finding the correct depth with top and bottom fixed floats. But they're a little heavy and make it difficult to cast waggler rigs. A smaller pole plummet may be better here, or some anglers pinch a large split shot on the bend of the hook.

You may have a good idea which part of the swim you intend to fish, but when plumbing-up, it's a good idea to try and build up a mental picture of the bottom terrain over the swim as a whole.

This way you won't miss hidden features like shelves and depressions, which might hold a good head of fish,

Above: **Traditional cork, Image brass and clip-on plummets.**

Right: **Plumbing the swim**

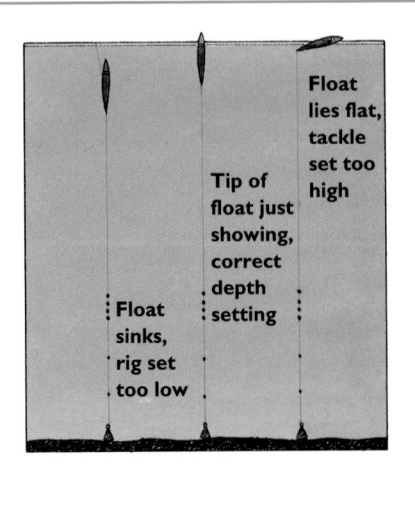

maybe just a few feet away from where you first intended to try. Extensive plumbing will also reveal any underwater weed beds and it's crucial you know where these are, so you can steer big fish around them.

It's normal practice to begin a session with your hookbait presented just on, or just off the bottom. To find the exact depth you need to make a rough guess to begin with and try an experimental cast. If the float sinks out of sight you will know the rig isn't set deep enough. Retrieve the tackle and slide the float up the line by a foot or so. Keep

doing this until the float bobs up, remembering to leave the reel line slack or you'll get a false reading.

If you have set your float too high, it will lie flat on the surface, or stand too proud. This is because dropper shot are lying on the bottom. In this instance you will have to keep sliding the float down the line, until only the very tip shows.

Once you are happy that the plummet is resting on the bottom and just the float tip is showing, you have the rig set at the correct depth and can start fishing with confidence.

BOMBS AND FEEDERS

Arlesey bombs vary in size for a given weight depending on the density of non-toxic material.

The float won't always bring you the best results. Sometimes the fish require a static bait and this isn't always possible to achieve with float tackle.

Also, the fish could be beyond the range of your float rigs, or maybe the conditions make it too difficult to present a float properly. That's the moment to consider using either the leger or swimfeeder.

Arlesey bombs are the most popular and streamlined leger weights. They are suitable for both light legering and long range specimen fishing. They begin at 1/8oz and are now made from non-toxic alloys up to an ounce. Larger versions are still made from lead.

Bream anglers particularly favour this type of weight, because it casts accurately and doesn't make a lot of disturbance over shallow water.

Light leger rigs are normally fished within range of loose feed. They work well in their own right, but this is also a good option to try after a swim has been 'fished out' with float tackle. It's surprising how a static bait can bring new life to a swim after it has apparently dried up.

Heavier leger rigs are extensively used by carp anglers. It's possible to loose feed boilies over great distances, into open water, or towards fishy looking features such as distant islands. It's a very productive method.

Another popular long range legering method, is to fish over a bed of groundbait laced with attractive feed like casters, hemp and squatts. Balls of groundbait can be fed accurately up to 70 yards by catapult and it's a very good method for catching bream, tench and smaller carp.

TYPES OF FEEDER

Straight leger tackle won't always bring the best response. Flow rates might make it difficult to get loose feed in the right place, or the fish may want more regular, smaller amounts of feed. In these cases, the swimfeeder is a potentially productive method.

Open-end feeders are designed to take groundbait in varying consistences to suit the type of water being fished. Groundbait can be used neat, if you feel the fish don't want a lot of feed, or when simple baits like bread are used and you don't want to confuse the fish with lots of other offerings.

But one of the most telling open-end feeder tactics, on both rivers and stillwaters, is to use minimal groundbait. In this case it's simply a holding medium, so the feeder can be packed out with tasty tempters like casters, hemp, squatts, pinkies, chopped worm, sweetcorn...the list is almost endless.

The feeder is often positioned quite close to the hookbait. This guarantees free offerings are deposited around it on every cast.

There are several open-end designs to choose from. Some have heavy weights for distance, or fast water work. Others are lighter and designed to lift up quickly off the bottom on the retrieve to stop them snagging in weedy or rocks.

Most open-enders are constructed with perspex bodies, but there are also cage designs, made from wire, or plastic mesh. These are useful in gaining improved cloud effects from wetter, or very dry groundbait mixes.

Blockend feeders come into play when you suspect groundbait won't have any beneficial effects. These tend to work best on rivers, but will still have the odd good day on stillwaters. They are primarily designed for use with neat maggots, but also work well, packed with casters and hemp.

Large maggot feeders are productive on rivers holding a big head of chub and barbel. To draw and keep these hungry fish interested, it's possible to get through nearly a gallon of maggots in a

Above: **Open-ended feeders made from perspex with side weights.**

Left: **Cage feeders produce improved cloud effects.**

Below: **Thamesley and Storey blockends. They're mainly used with neat maggots.**

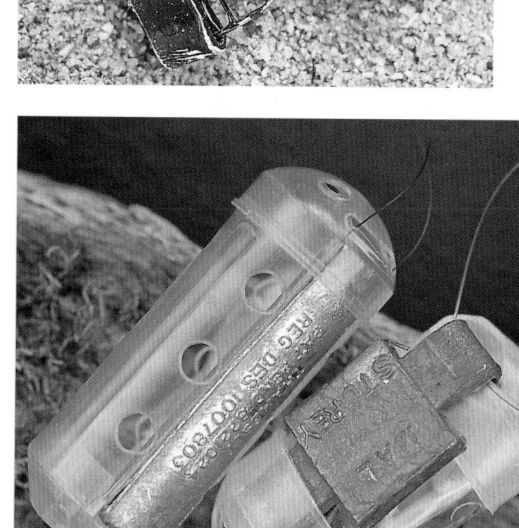

Versatile blockends with inter-changeable weights.

Springtip shows up very delicate touches.

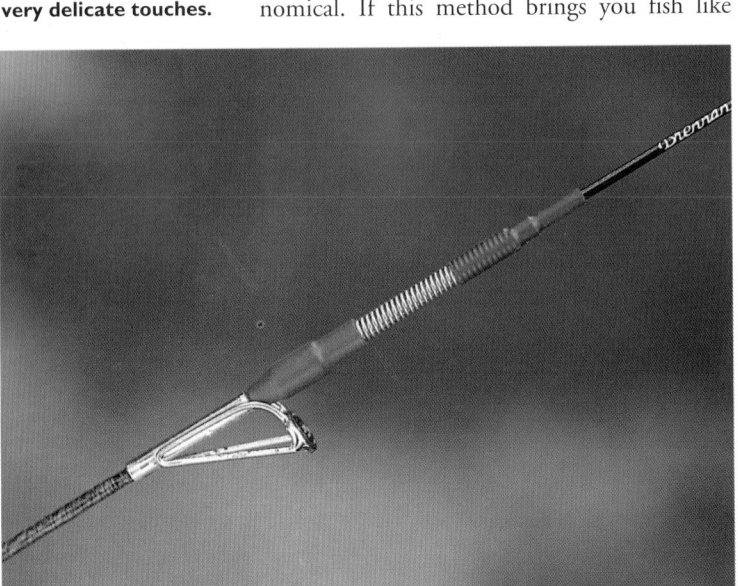

bream, roach and hybrids, you've probably got the choice right.

On a river venue, the open-end feeder can bring a fast response, then fade rapidly. It could be there's no bream around and if you have caught odd small chub, this will tell you it's time to switch to the blockend design.

Some blockend feeders have inter-changeable weights. This is a good feature, so if flow rates pick up, or a longer cast is required, you can alter the rig very quickly.

Another point to watch, is the size of the holes in the body of feeders. This isn't crucial with open-enders, but a blockend with too small exit holes, won't release the feed fast enough in many situations. It's possible to purchase a small plastic tool which will enlarge feeder holes.

When casting long range, the reverse may apply. Lively maggots soon wriggle out of a feeder, even while you're getting positioned correctly to launch it out. In this case, you may need to cover the lower exit holes with some waterproof electrical tape, or fill them with special feeder plugs.

long session. But don't worry, there will be just as many days when a smaller feeder scores well!

On hard winter days it's often better to go easy with the feed. A small link feeder, fished at long range to far bank cover, often produces big catches of chub. Closer in, the method also tempts big roach and perch.

Selecting the correct type of feeder comes with experience. But if you're unsure, start on the open-ender, if only because it's more economical. If this method brings you fish like

BITE INDICATORS

Quiver, spring and swingtips are the main bite indicators used when legering, or feeder fishing. The quivertips are the most popular and easy devices to use, and these can be screwed into a threaded top eye. However, many specialist leger and feeder rods now come with several plug-in versions.

Quivertips are graded by test curves. They go down to very sensitive 0.50 oz and 0.75 oz models for spotting delicate stillwater bites. The 1 oz to 2 oz tips are used at long range in stillwaters, or on medium paced rivers while 3 oz to 4 oz tips are for fast flow rates.

Springtips usually have dual settings. In one mode they work like a conventional quivertip, but they have the added facility of a special housing, which when unlocked, brings a much more sensitive spring into play. The tip shows up very delicate touches when used on the spring and is worth trying on difficult stillwaters and slow flowing rivers.

The swingtip offers less resistance than the other two major forms of bite indication. This makes it popular for breaming methods on stillwaters. In order to combat surface drift, weights can be added to the end of swingtips, which normally hang loose on a length of silicone tubing. There's also specially stiffened, moulded rubber housings, which can be fitted to some swingtips. Apart from making them more effective in drift, this also makes it possible to use them on medium paced rivers.

For stillwaters, an electronic bite indicator which registers any slight movement on the line, takes some of the strain out of keeping your eyes glued to a quivertip. Some indicators rely on a basic antenna connected to contacts and against which the line tightens to complete the circuit and sound the alarm. With more sophisticated models, the line rests on a revolving wheel and any movement cuts through an internal photo electric cell to register a bleep and activate light emitting diodes.

Electronic indicators are essential for long sessions on the bank – chiefly for specimen sized fish. They're almost always set up with a monkey climber which comprises an indicator clipped on the line and suspended on a vertical steel needle for stability in wind. A popular alternative to monkey climbers are Swingers which fit on the front bank stick below the electronic indicator and hang from the line by way of a metal arm and line clip. A movable weight permits variation of the resistance to defeat surface drift or wind and the Swinger falls free once a run pulls line from the clip.

Left: Swingtip - effective for bream on stillwaters.

Below: Swinger indicators with electronic bite alarms and stable rod pod – a favourite set-up for carp.

BASIC TACKLE SET-UPS

Opposite: The bodied waggler has done its job and another bream hits the net.

FLOAT RIGS

There are numerous ways of shotting up a float but newcomers should first gain confidence with the basic, well tried set-ups. Simple shotting arrangements are less prone to tangles. More complicated ones may sometimes catch you more fish, but not if your tackle is out of the water, more than it is in! Well balanced rigs are absolutely essential if you are going to master casting techniques and general handling of the tackle.

STICKS

There are two basic shotting-up systems for stick floats. Many anglers start the session with strung shotting. This involves evenly spacing small, or medium sized shot between the float and hook. Most stick designs are marked with their capacities – classic examples are four No.4 and six No.6.

This doesn't mean you must slavishly follow these formats because floats are rarely marked to their exact capacities. Often, with a four No.4 model, the manufacturer will have left room to add a couple of No.8 shot to dot it down cor-

Bulk and strung stick

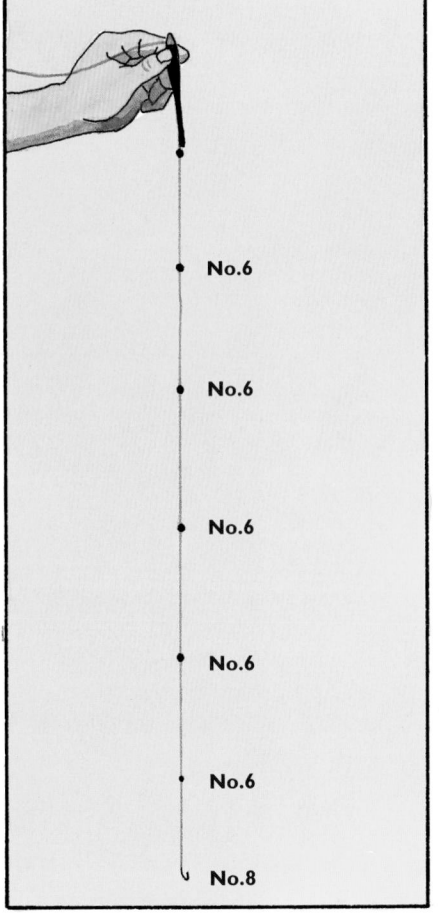

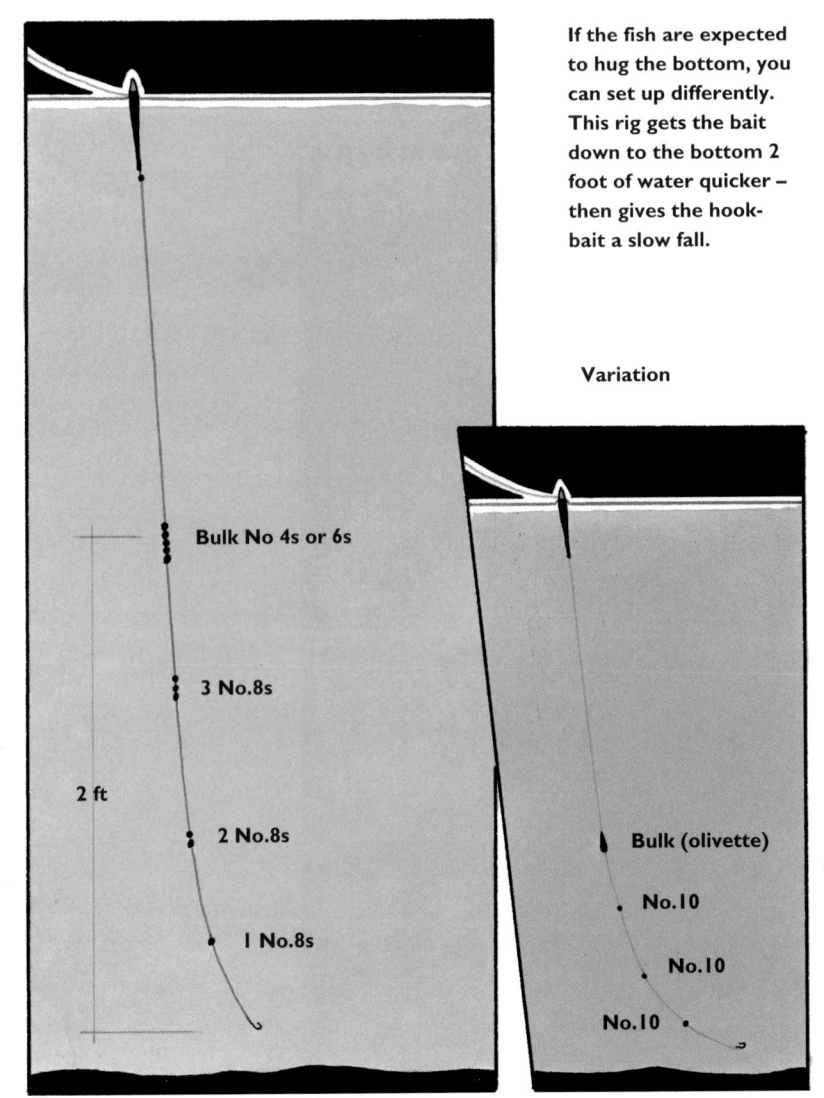

If the fish are expected to hug the bottom, you can set up differently. This rig gets the bait down to the bottom 2 foot of water quicker – then gives the hook-bait a slow fall.

Variation

rectly. This is useful because one of these No.8s can be fixed under the float to act as a marker while the other serves as a dropper shot, nearest the hook.

In a swim approximately four feet deep, a stick float carrying four spread out No.4 shot and a No.8 dropper will perform quite well. But in deeper water, say eight feet, the spacings between this minimal amount of shot will be too great and the rig won't cast very smoothly.

In this case it would be more practical to reduce the gaps by switching to No. 6 shot. This gives eight smaller shot to play around with down the line, possibly even ten if the float will also take a couple of No.8s as marker and dropper shot.

When spreading shot, try to pick a mid-range size which will give you six to ten inch gaps, evenly spaced down the rig. Fixed in this way, the set-up is more streamlined and therefore easier to cast out in a straight line. This is one of the very few instances where more shot will not cause tangles.

The other option in deeper water – if you don't want to greatly increase the amount of shot you use – is to begin spreading them with smaller gaps, from half depth downwards.

Spread shot arrangements are very versatile. They take fish both on-the-drop and from different levels, including the bottom, as the rig trots through the swim. Spread shot also offer the option of bulking them together, should the fish show a preference for more bottom presented baits.

Bulk shotted sticks get the hookbait down fast when small fish attack it before it has a chance to tempt bites from better quality samples. This kind of set-up may also perform well if the fish won't budge from the bottom, or if the swim is a bit pacey.

Usually, the bulk is fixed 2–3 feet above the hook, with between one and three smaller dropper shot spread out below.

Use small weights as bulk, if you wish to retain the option of quickly altering the rig to fish spread shot. That allows you to respond immediately by shuffling the shot if the fish start competing for feed up in the water. Or it is possible to use larger number No.1s or BBs.

When rivers are pushing hard, experienced anglers often get a sixth sense feeling that the fish won't accept baits off the bottom, so they use a more streamlined olivette as bulk.

Bulk shotted rigs are easy to cast by flicking out underarm. But don't get into the habit of using them because of this slight advantage alone. They are not always right.

There is also a good case for using very small strung-out shot in some situations with lighter stick rigs. At first sight it may appear over-complicated to string lots of tiny No.8s down the line, but when flow rates are minimal, this trick will help to pull the rig through better than a few larger shot might achieve.

BALSAS

Balsas are a natural progression up from sticks when the water is pulling a bit hard, or is too deep for light shotting. These floats take quite a lot more weight size for size.

It is possible to string out larger shot, such as No.4s, or No. 1s with this type of float, but more

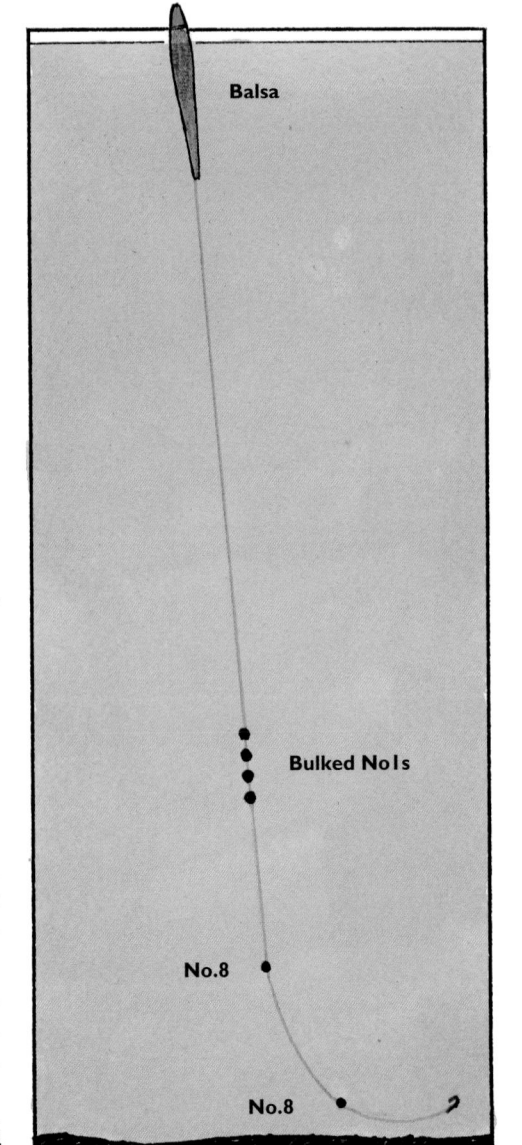

often they work best with a bulk weight. Number 1s, or BBs are favourite here, then it's a good idea to taper shot sizes towards the hook to keep the rig balanced.

After the bulk, a typical balsa rig might have a No.4 shot ten inches below, a No.6 the same distance below that and finish with a No.8 shot as the final dropper.

Always keep bulked shot below half depth and you almost certainly won't experience any tangles on the cast.

CHUBBERS

These large capacity floats are always used with a main bulk. To further simplify the rig and minimalise tangles, it's a good idea to match up a large olivette to chubbers. Once you have this

fixed on the line, just one or two dropper shot, usually No.4s or No.1s are needed to complete the set-up.

For long casts it's best to position the bulk quite close to the hook, probably about 20–30 inches away.

STRAIGHT WAGGLERS

With any bottom-end attached float, it's advisable to place at least two thirds of the weight capacity around its base. This insures it will always precede the rest of the rig in flight, gaining good distance and accuracy. If you try balancing a float's loading equally between locking shot and those spread down the line, it will almost certainly cartwheel on the cast and cause all sorts of problems.

The straight is used in medium to fast flows, where the hookbait is wanted down fast.

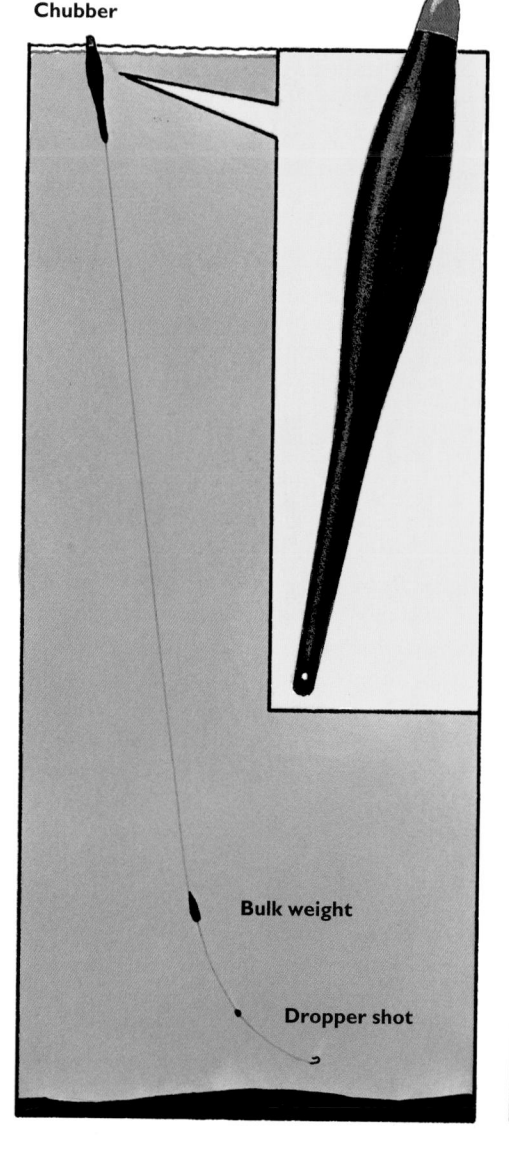

Chubber

Bulk weight

Dropper shot

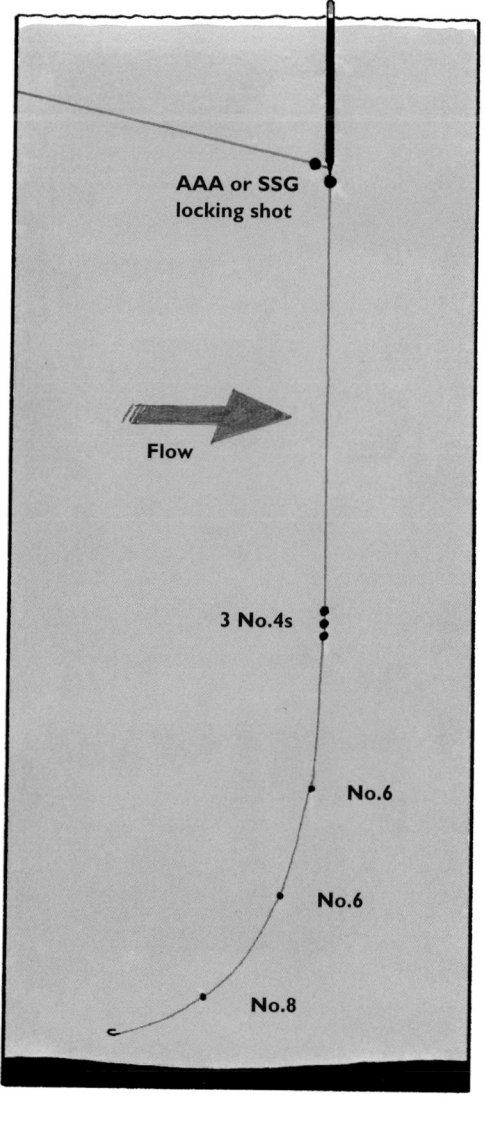

Straight

AAA or SSG locking shot

Flow

3 No.4s

No.6

No.6

No.8

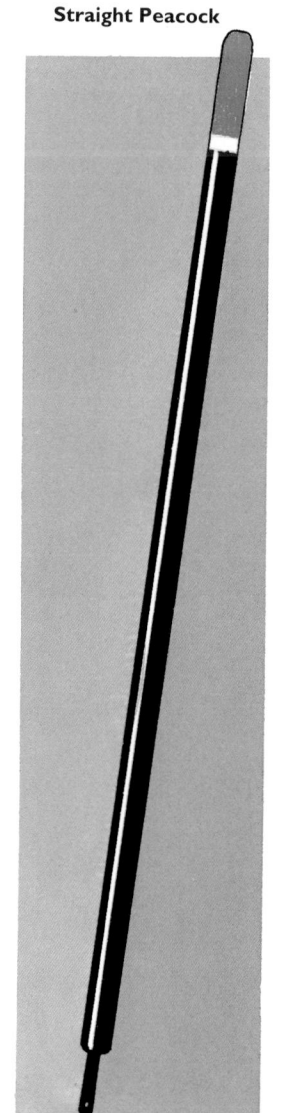

Straight Peacock

Fixing a heavier shot loading down the line instead of around the base of the float impairs accuracy and halves the casting distance.

The crucial rule which must be observed with properly loaded wagglers, is to feather the reel line with your fingers, just before the rig lands. The main shotting around the float propels it out, but you must prevent the lighter shot following behind, wrapping around the reel line above the float as it lands.

If you feather the reel line correctly, the float touches down very lightly on the surface. This is a good thing in itself, but most importantly, the end tackle will overtake the float and land in a neat straight line in front of it. You probably won't get any tangles once you've mastered this simple technique.

For flowing water, once a straight waggler has been locked on the line with two-thirds of its capacity, the remainder of the loading can be utilised as spread, or perhaps semi-bulked smaller shot.

Shotting down the rig is, in fact, very similar to that of a stick float.

If the fish are taking up in the water, more shot can be used around the float, so only a few small shot are spread down the rig. This gives the hookbait a slow, enticing fall. Number 8s and No. 10s are the favourites for this set-up, using just two or three spread evenly from just below half depth.

On stillwaters, it's rare that a lot of shot will be needed down the rig with a straight waggler, unless small fish are a problem in the upper layers. Generally, in this situation, a straight waggler would be used to drag a bait over-depth. Three or four No.8 or 10 shot spread over the last four feet of the rig should achieve the right setting. A couple of the lower shot can actually be used to drag on the bottom where they will act as a brake.

INSERT WAGGLERS

Most of the time, very light shot are used down the rig with insert wagglers. These floats perform well when the fish are taking baits off bottom. When that happens, most of the float's loading is used to lock it on the line. Perhaps only three No.10 shot might be required to give the hookbait a slow fall.

On calm, shallow stillwaters the same format often gives options of fishing on-the-drop and on the bottom – should the hookbait get that far without a response.

If the float begins to drag out of position, you may need to alter the shotting to slightly more substantial No.8s.

Inserts can also be used with a light bulk, maybe three or four No.8s set three feet from the hook and a couple of No.10s spread out below.

These are the best floats when you're looking for spot-on accuracy, such as when casting tight to far bank cover. This is the only time with a waggler rig where the reel line isn't feathered hard. The idea is to get the float as tight in to the cover as possible.

If you feather the rig properly here, the end tackle will end up snagged in the bushes and trees. You can risk a straight cast to the desired spot, or just lightly dab the reel line at the last moment, so the lower part of the rig falls to the side of the float.

Inserts are better for more delicate on-the-drop or off-bottom bites.

Insert Peacock or Reed.

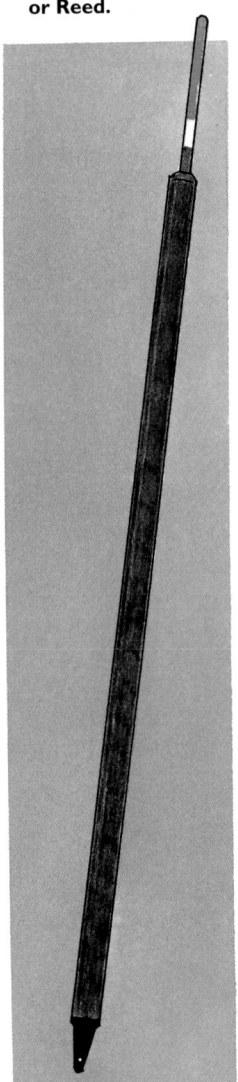

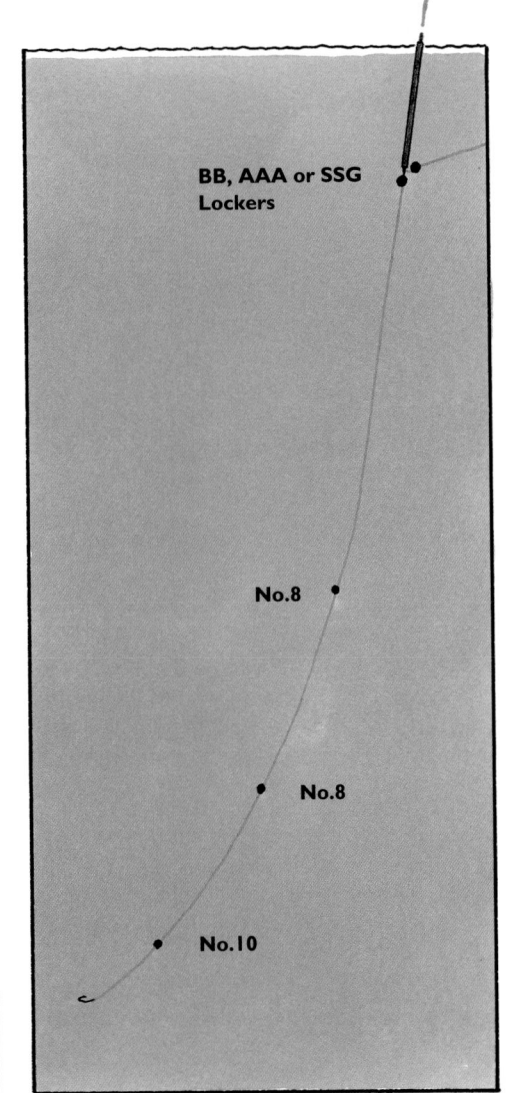

BB, AAA or SSG Lockers

No.8

No.8

No.10

BODIED WAGGLERS

These should be looked upon as extensions of straight and insert wagglers. The body at the base allows more casting weight to be added for greater distances. Shotting formats down the line are similar.

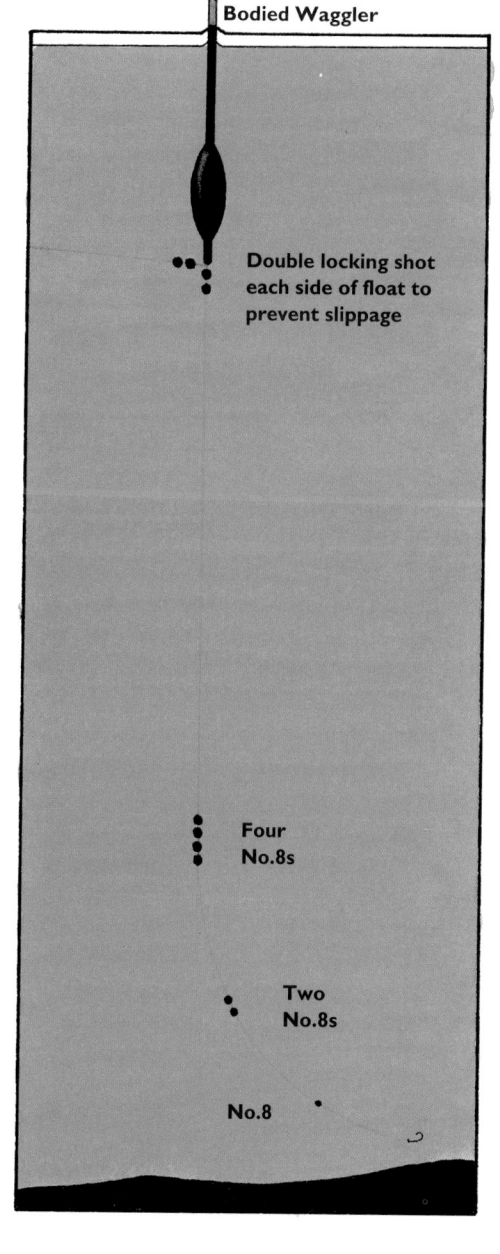

Bodied Waggler

Double locking shot each side of float to prevent slippage

Four No.8s

Two No.8s

No.8

QUILLS

These are best used close-in with very minimal shot. A favourite method is to anchor one large shot on the bottom with the float set over-depth by about 20 inches. The rod tip is sunk and the line is tightened up, so just the tip of the quill is left showing. A bite usually registers by the float lifting as a fish picks up the hookbait and with it the anchor shot.

SLIDERS

These specialist floats require some form of bulk shotting in order to pull the line through to the stop knot.

Top and bottom sliders have a main bulk set approximately 3–4 feet from the hook and one or two dropper shot spread below this. Large shot like No.1s, BBs and AAAs are used for bulk, and an olivette is also passable. Droppers are usually quite big No.4s or 1s.

The majority of bottom-end sliders are normally semi-loaded. This helps cock the float quickly so line runs smoothly through the base

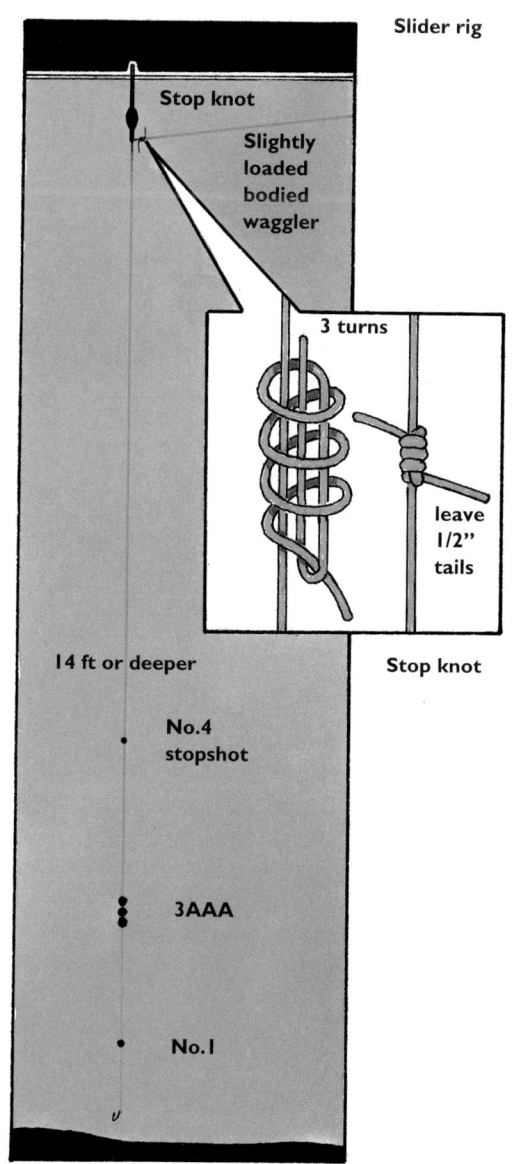

Slider rig

Stop knot

Slightly loaded bodied waggler

3 turns

leave 1/2" tails

14 ft or deeper

Stop knot

No.4 stopshot

3AAA

No.1

Sliding rubber float stops.

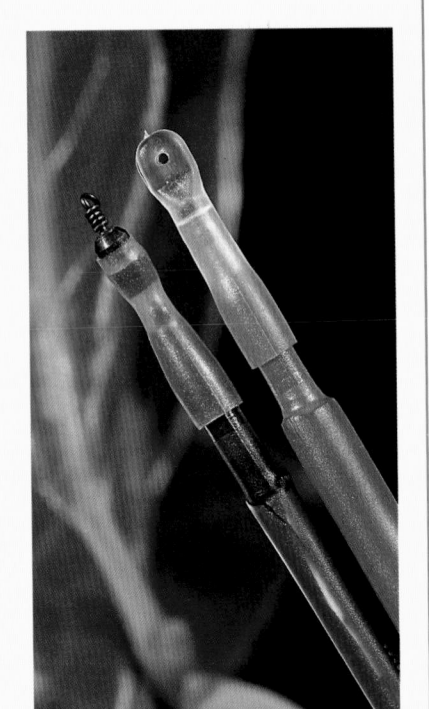

eye. These require smaller bulks comprising No.1s or BB shot. Droppers are No.4s or No.1s (often just one).

A good trick to prevent tangles with both types of slider is to position a No.6 shot several feet above the bulk. This stops the float from tangling with it and the hooklength on the cast. It's vital the distance between this upper shot is greater than the distance between the bulk weighting and the hook.

Bottom-end sliders can also be cast from a position where they are resting on the bulk shot. This gains far greater casting distance because the loaded float and bulk weight fly out together. But it's a difficult set-up to work with and tangles are always possible. The rig must be feathered before it touches down and even then in gusting winds the hooklength has an annoying tendency to wrap itself around the bulk shot.

Because sliders are deep water floats, the stop knot will often have to travel through the rod rings. This means leaving at least half-inch ends of line after the knot is formed and tightened, otherwise it will snag. It's best to use 3 lb line to form this knot, anything thinner might force its way through the slider float's eye.

If you don't fancy tying slider knots, it's possible to purchase sliding float stops made from small beads of soft rubber. These come on wire or nylon loops and are easily transferred to the reel line, before setting up the tackle. The reel line is threaded through the wire loop and brought back on itself. One of the rubber stops is then slid off the wire and onto the reel line, where it can now be further advanced up the

---

FLOAT ATTACHMENTS

Top and bottom floats like sticks are fixed to the line with float rubbers. It's better to ignore the base eye on most models. Instead, you should thread three rubbers on the line and fix the stick into them so the top rubber – usually the largest – is approximately half an inch from the top of the float. The next rubber is positioned at the top of the float's stem and the final one – normally the smallest – fits at the base of the stem.

Apart from making the float more secure, fishing with three rubbers provides a spare already installed on the line should the top one split.

Wagglers are best attached to the reel line with an adaptor which pushes onto the base of the float. There are several types, including pure silicone, swivel, and wire and silicone models. They're a more versatile method than feeding the line directly through the float's base eye because it becomes possible to swap floats without breaking the rig down.

This quick-change facility is often needed, as conditions can alter and a smaller or larger float may be required in a hurry.

Silicone adaptors suit floats carrying up to 3AAA capacity. Swivel, or wire waggler links are better for larger floats, because the line won't cut through them. Some specialist canal floats have swivel adaptors designed to fit base pegs without an attachment eye.

Waggler adaptors – Middy River and Drennan Silicone.

line, above the short piece which was first doubled back.

Some anglers prefer to use two of these stops together to prevent slippage.

CANAL WAGGLERS

Canal wagglers are scaled down in size, because casting distances may only be 10 to 15 metres and the venues are mainly shallow. Some canal floats are simply smaller versions of insert wagglers, made from peacock, clear plastic, or reed. But most popular nowadays are the more gradually tapering all-balsa designs.

Whichever canal waggler you select, one common characteristic lies in shotting patterns. Most shot goes around the float, with perhaps only two or three No.10 shot, or even smaller micro shot spread out as droppers. Some canal regulars use tiny No.7 or 8 Styl weights, because these give the hookbait an even slower fall rate.

Most canal wagglers take between a couple of No.1 shot and two AAA as lockers.

LEGER RIGS

Many anglers experience lots of tangles when first trying to use leger tackle and yet with a little thought, it's possible to arrive at quite basic rigs which will hardly ever give any trouble.

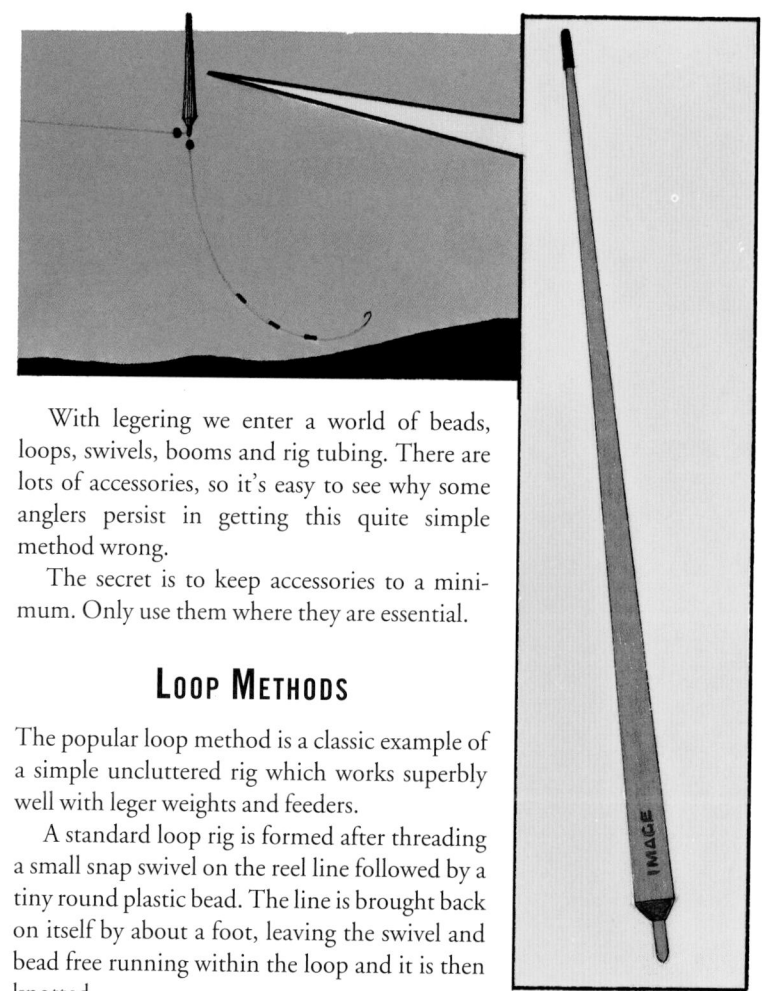

With legering we enter a world of beads, loops, swivels, booms and rig tubing. There are lots of accessories, so it's easy to see why some anglers persist in getting this quite simple method wrong.

The secret is to keep accessories to a minimum. Only use them where they are essential.

LOOP METHODS

The popular loop method is a classic example of a simple uncluttered rig which works superbly well with leger weights and feeders.

A standard loop rig is formed after threading a small snap swivel on the reel line followed by a tiny round plastic bead. The line is brought back on itself by about a foot, leaving the swivel and bead free running within the loop and it is then knotted.

At the base of the large loop, a smaller one

Above: **Canal waggler**

Left: **Loop rigs**

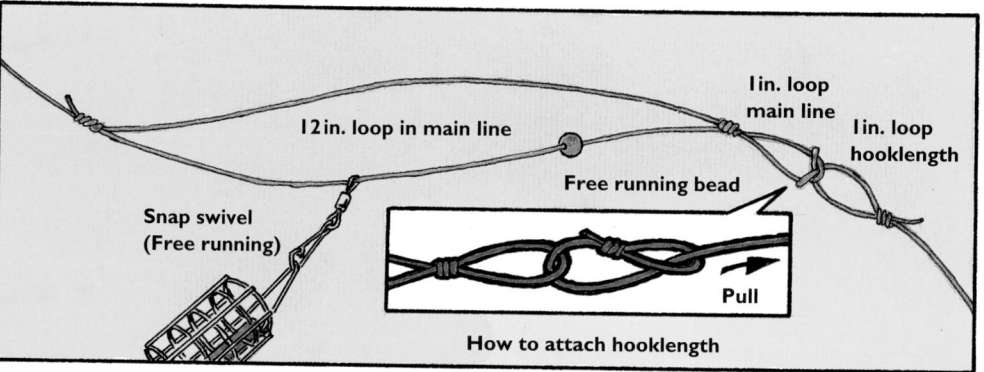

Snap swivel
(Free running)

12 in. loop in main line

Free running bead

1 in. loop
main line

1 in. loop
hooklength

Pull

How to attach hooklength

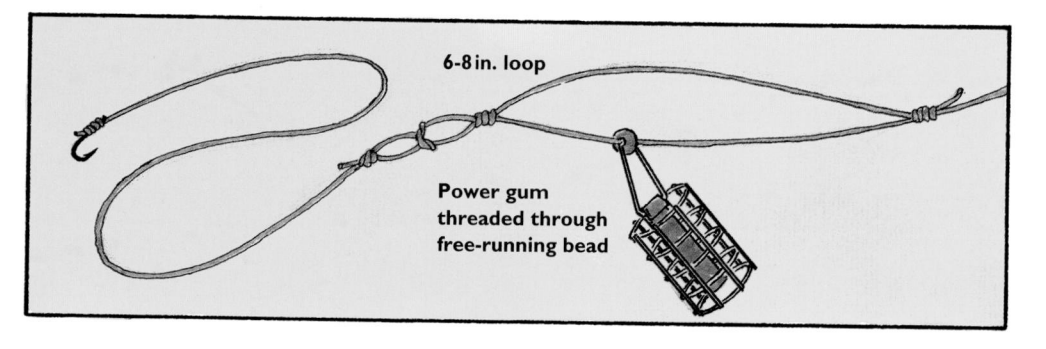

6-8 in. loop

Power gum
threaded through
free-running bead

Right: **Feeder modified with Powergum link.**

Far right: **Snap swivel.**

Far right: **Drennan swivel bead with sheath of silicone covering the snap swivel to prevent tangles.**

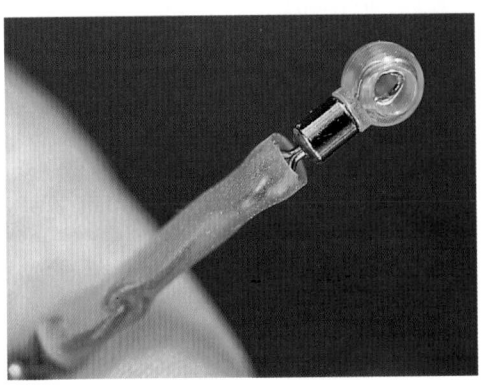

inch loop is formed, to which the hooklength is eventually attached. At this stage it's easy to see why the bead is there – it stops the swivel from jamming, or over-riding the smaller loop knot.

Once a leger weight, or feeder is clipped to the snap swivel, the extra weight pushes against the smaller loop, sending it out to the side. This in turn keeps the hooklength away from the rest of the tackle on the cast. Tangles are very rare with this set-up and although the leger, or feeder is trapped, bites are still very confident.

It is possible to simplify the loop method further by specially fitting your feeders with Powergum links, which have a small bead ready installed on them. The reel line is threaded through the bead and a small loop is formed, so just the bead and feeder is running in it. A smaller loop is formed again to take the hooklength and you are left with a very good river feeder rig. Some anglers shorten the loop on which the feeder is running to just a few inches if bites are difficult to hit. This often causes the fish to dislodge the feeder and hook themselves.

FREE-RUNNING LEGER

A good basic rig to try with a bead is a free running leger. An Arlesey bomb is either threaded direct on the line, or clipped to a swivel link first. Next, a small bead is threaded on and then the end of the reel line is formed into a small loop to attach the hooklength. A small shot, or leger stop is positioned directly above this loop to hold the

leger weight away from the hooklength.

To simplify this rig even further, a specially designed sliding bead replaces both the original one and the snap swivel and the weight is fixed direct to this.

The basic running leger used by carp anglers features a hook link formed from nylon or braid with a swivel for attachment to the main line. This swivel acts as the stop against which a rubber buffer bead rests to prevent the bomb chaffing the knot.

Shorter links of possibly six or eight inches are preferable for hard bottomed waters.

Free-running leger.

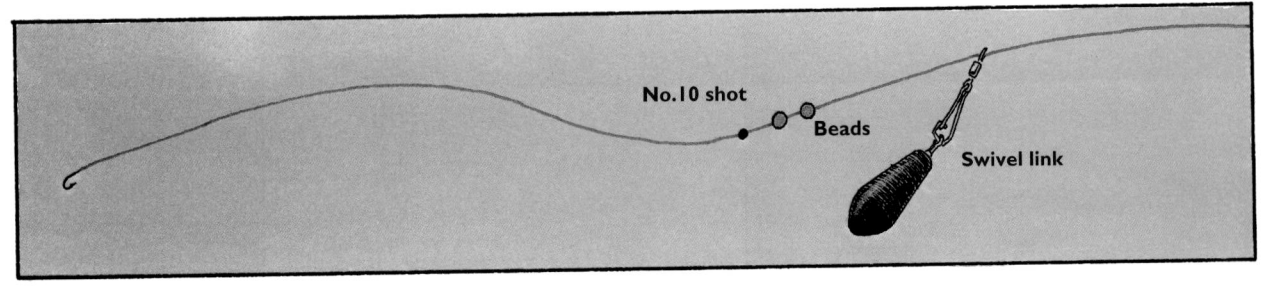

No.10 shot

Beads

Swivel link

PATERNOSTER

This is the most simple leger rig. The bomb or feeder is tied direct to the end of the reel line, then six to 12 inches back up the line a tiny loop is formed on which the hooklength is fixed.

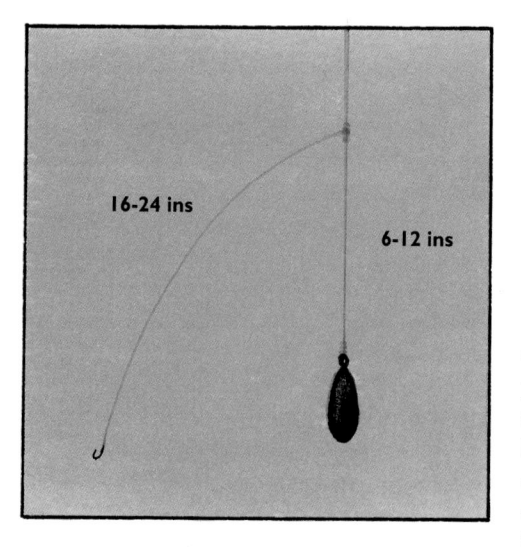

16-24 ins

6-12 ins

HELICOPTER RIG

When carp become suspicious of long rig tube set-ups, the helicopter or rotary rig will also prevent soft, braided hook links from tangling. Numerous systems have been developed but the basic idea remains the same. The weight is tied directly to the end of the line and a swivel bead with the hook link attached rests directly above this with beads either side for easy rotation. The beads are trapped in position with rubber float stops. Other, purpose-made systems eliminate

the float stops by simply incorporating a length of silicone tubing which fixes on the swivel eye of the bomb.

LEGER COMPONENTS

BOOMS Some anglers use short plastic tube booms to keep the hooklength away from their feeder rigs, but in reality this only works when casting over short ranges. They're sold with bead and clip ready installed and usually have a good diagram on the packaging explaining how to set them up.

RIG TUBE Soft silicone tubing is useful for partly covering swivels and nylon links on feeders. It stops the hooklength from tangling back around the feeder. Long, stiff lengths of tubing are also regularly used by specimen anglers to prevent hook links of soft, limp braid tangling around the weight and line when hurled over long distances. They often thread the line through 12 to 20 inches of fine, stiff tubing which critically must be at least a third longer in length than the hook link itself. The leger weight is then hung on a swivel bead which fits tightly on the tube.

SWIVELS Standard barrel swivels can be used on feeder links, but most feeder manufacturers now fit their products with diamond eye swivels. These have a more pointed eye, which hangs and anchors a knot better.

Swivel links, also known as American snap swivels, are popular for attaching leger weights and feeders to rigs. They offer a useful quick change facility.

Helicopter rig.

NETTING FISH

After you have mastered getting the tackle out cleanly and begin to catch better sized fish, there is a simple netting procedure to follow. As the fish nears the bank, you should position your landing net directly out in front of you and submerge the net. It is very important to bring fish in over the net, never try to chase the fish around with it.

If you try to hurry the fish in, by following it with the net, you risk spooking the fish, or bumping it off the hook.

Silicone float rubbers, leger stops and swivels.

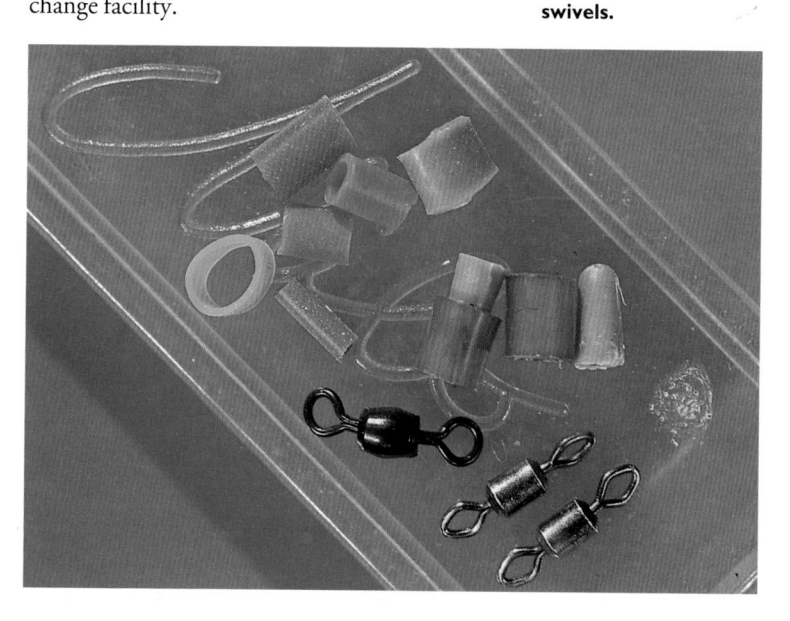

LEGER STOPS These come in two sizes. They consist of a plastic peg, which pushes into a ring. This locks the device and is more secure than relying on a split shot. It's advisable to only use leger stops on reel lines over 3 lb, because they can pinch and damage finer monofilament.

CASTING TECHNIQUES

There are three main casting styles. The overhead is most frequently used by anglers, but bankside terrain doesn't always make this practi-cal. Therefore, underarm and sideways casts must also be mastered. The sideways action is often a better way of casting tackle underneath far bank cover.

OVERHEAD It's best to learn the basics of overhead casting from a stationary position. This technique is good for both leger and float tackle. The tackle is brought over your head and held still, with the rod pointing backwards at approximately 10 o'clock. At this stage, it's best to focus on your target, then the rod is propelled sharply forward, over your head and the tackle released at 2 o'clock.

It requires practise to get the hang of the timing involved here and it might be easier to try the technique with a small leger weight first – if only to sort out a rhythm and work out the crucial rod positioning.

As experience is gained, it's possible to bring the rod back and then forward to make the cast in one movement. If the bankside behind allows, it may also be feasible to bring the rod even lower, to gain a greater casting arc and, therefore, better distance.

Below: **Eyes focused on the target for the overhead cast.**

Below right: **Overhead cast.**

Bottom: **Underarm cast.**

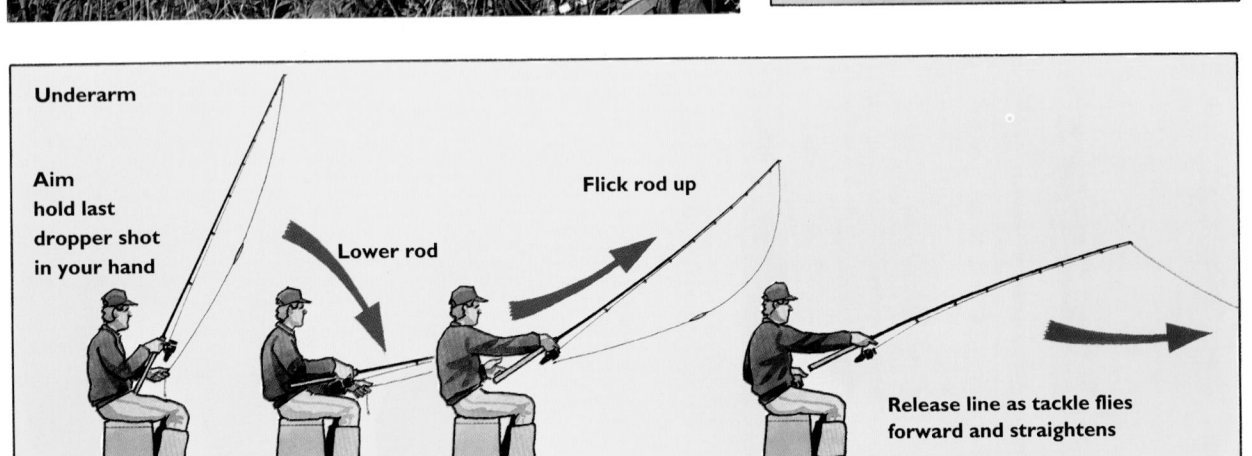
Overhead

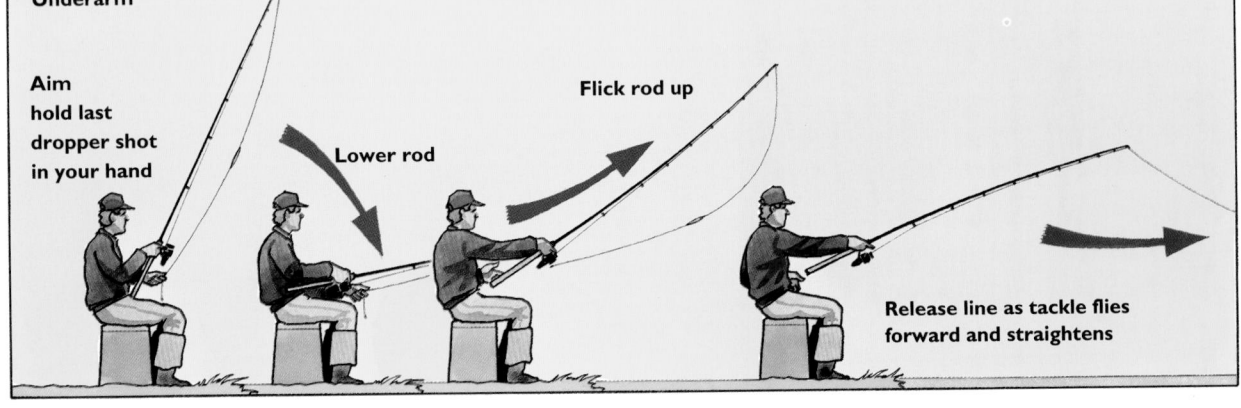
Underarm

Aim hold last dropper shot in your hand

Lower rod

Flick rod up

Release line as tackle flies forward and straightens

UNDERARM The underarm technique only works with bulk shotted rigs and strung stick float formats. Here, the hooklength is lightly held between the index finger and thumb of your free hand, just above the hook. The rod is brought low to the water and then flicked sharply upwards, at the same time releasing the rig from your free hand.

The weight of the shot causes the lower end of the rig to lead out in front of the float and after you have practised a little, it should go in a straight line.

SIDEWAYS Sideways casts are performed in similar fashion to the underarm. Again, you should try to hold the line with your free hand – if it's possible to sweep the rod around from that side of your body.

If the rod can only be brought around from the other side, the rig is left hanging free, with about three feet of line between its tip and the float. This manoeuvre only tends to work with shallow set floats and the rod has to be brought back and then forward in one smooth movement, to prevent the end tackle from snagging the ground.

This cast can be used to skim light waggler rigs under overhanging foliage on the far bank of small rivers and canals. It's a deadly way of catching chub and carp, species which like to hug cover very tightly.

POINTS TO REMEMBER

The most accurate cast is overhead, or very slightly to one side. This is the only way to properly launch feeder tackle, or heavier leger weights. It's also an accurate way of casting wagglers and big stick floats into open water.

Most top and bottom fixed floats can be cast underarm, but this isn't a successful method for the waggler.

The sideways cast is used with top and bottom float designs, but is normally associated with waggler tackle. Good timing, when releasing the tackle, is the only way to gain the necessary accuracy with this cast and the rod should end up pointing in the direction of the target area.

Casting out the tackle in a straight line using the underarm cast.

Sideways cast

Rod parallel to bank and kept low

Release last dropper shot as cast commences

Line release point

Sideways

SPECIES GUIDE

Principal fish features

Dorsal Fin · Dorsal Fin · Lateral line · Eye · Nostril · Caudal Fin · Anal Fin · Vent · Pectoral Fin · Gill cover · Pelvic Fin

Here's a checklist of the habitats, baits and British records for the most popular species in UK waters. Few anglers succeed in catching examples of every single species but in fishing you never know your luck!

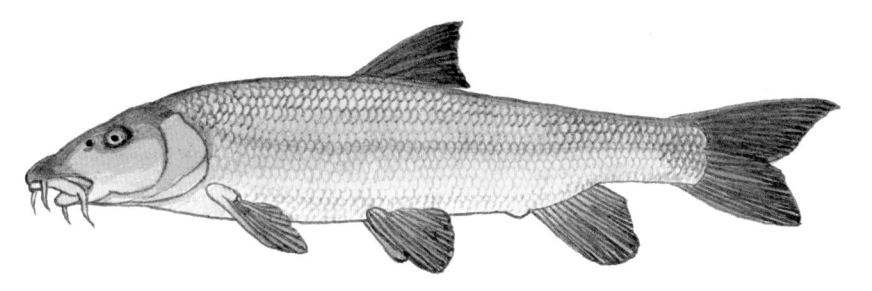

BARBEL

Barbel are a much sought after river species. On larger systems like the Severn and Trent they are prolific and relatively easy to catch while in the 1 lb to 5 lb bracket. They're primarily bottom feeders and keenly mop up small baits like maggots, hemp and casters. This makes the swimfeeder a deadly method. Big barbel are much more elusive and tend to be loners, or shoal with a handful of smaller fish.

Barbel are very powerful, streamlined fish, even a small three-pounder can prove more than a handful on standard tackle. They like fast water, especially over gravel runs and for this reason are often found in weirpools, in shallow weedy channels and swims which receive stronger flows such as on the outside of bends.

Deeper water is another place to look for this species. Barbel tend to hug any pronounced depressions in the river bed and seem to favour deep holes on the edge of faster water.

The maggot feeder is a popular method. Hemp and caster, packed into an open-end feeder, is another highly viable approach. A good bed of loose fed hemp, maggots, or casters can be put down closer in, and then fished over with a light link leger, or over-depth float rig.

Although barbel are caught on float tackle, presentation needs to be spot-on. It may involve using big floats and slowing the tackle right down so the hook bait is presented well on the bottom.

Another good way of taking them is to link leger with larger baits like luncheon meat, bread, sausage meat and sweetcorn. A roving approach pays dividends here, searching out weedy runs, letting a large bait trundle along the bottom and rest up momentarily against weed, or in slacks.

Barbel feed all year round, but best results are likely when rivers are carrying a bit of extra water, especially in late summer and autumn. In high summer when water levels may be quite low it's best to seek out more oxygenated water below weirs. In winter, deeper water usually proves more productive.

A barbel would be classed a specimen on most waters if it weighed over 9 lb.

BRITISH RECORD
15 lb 7 oz (7.002kg).

BLEAK

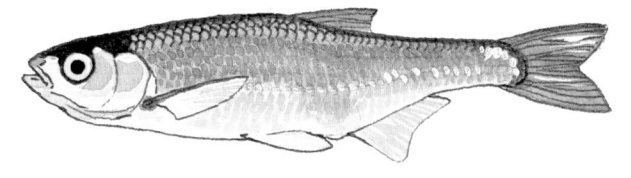

These small silver fish are surface feeders. They rarely exceed two ounces and can be a nuisance on larger rivers. They will greedily boil on the surface for loose fed baits like maggots and casters and strip soft hookbaits off the hook, often without registering a positive bite, even on float tackle. Sometimes anglers have to bulk shot their float rigs in order to get through hungry shoals of bleak, just so they can

BRONZE BREAM

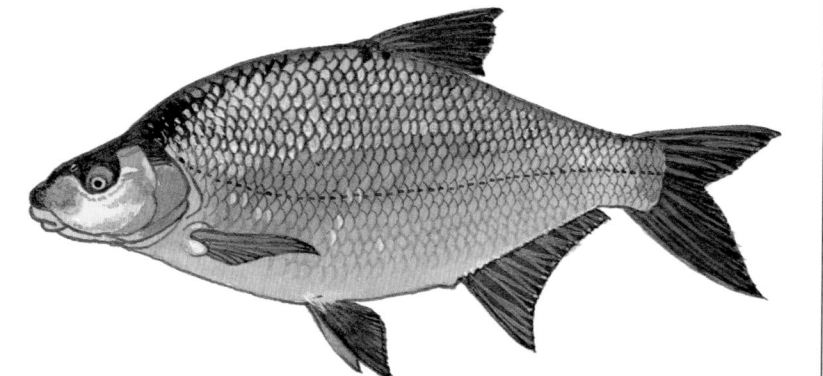

Larger common or bronze bream are thick-set fish. They are often described as slab-sided which explains the angler's affectionate nickname for them as slabs. Smaller bream up to 1 lb 8 oz tend to lie flat on the surface as they are played in towards the bank. It's often possible to skim them over the surface towards the landing net and this has led to another nickname, skimmers.

Bream are found in the majority of stillwaters and reach double-figures in large lakes, meres, pits and reservoirs. They also inhabit drains, fens and canals. Although many rivers also hold bream, they tend to be more localised.

Bream feed most avidly early, or late in the day, also at night and when the weather is humid and overcast. Generally they are bottom feeders, but they can sometimes be caught up in the water when conditions are particularly warm and bright.

Quiver and swingtipping are two of the most favoured breaming methods, combined with open-ended, groundbait feeders, or leger rigs.

Bream are shoal fish and often give away their presence by sending up strings of small bubbles, or by clouding shallow water as they graze along the bottom. Large bream also have a tendency to roll on the surface over feeding areas.

Noted bream hotspots on stillwaters are usually close to features such as gravel bars, islands, thick weed and lily beds, rush lined bays and inlets. They are often found in shallow to medium depths in summer, sometimes quite close to the bank. In winter they will move out into deeper open water.

Canal bream are often located in wide turning bays and where there are far bank features like rush beds, overhanging cover and moored boats.

River bream rarely move from noted areas. These are usually out of the main current and where the water is deeper.

This species responds well to groundbait and fair helpings of feed like casters, squatts and worms.

Bream can be fickle feeders. It's a good idea to change hookbaits regularly in the quest for bites. Red maggots, red and fluorescent coloured pinkies, casters, worms, sweetcorn and bread all have their day. This fish has a liking for cocktail baits, such as worm and caster or maggot and caster. Coloured maggot combinations, including reds, whites, yellows and bronzes are also worth trying.

Some anglers even breed their own hooker maggots for bream fishing. These are called gozzers and are larger and softer skinned than commercial shop bought bait.

A big catch of bream would normally comprise fish in the 2 lb to 5 lb category but fish up to 7 lb are not uncommon. A double-figure fish would be classed a specimen.

Silver bream are much smaller than the common variety and its distribution is limited to the south and east of England. It is easily confused with small common bream and scale counts might be necessary to differentiate the species. The British record stands at just 15 oz and reflects the uncertainty surrounding the identification of silvers.

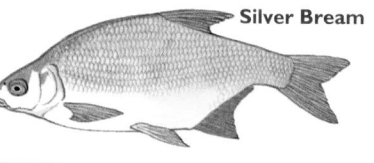
Silver Bream

BRITISH RECORDS
bronze 16 lb 9 oz (7.512 kg)
and silver 15 oz (0.425 kg).

get at the bigger, bottom feeding fish.

Matchmen are probably the only anglers who might consider bleak as a serious proposition. Some top stars have become very proficient at whipping out literally hundreds of bleak on scaled down surface pole rigs and they may catch well over 1,000 during the course of a five hour competition.

Bleak are mainly found in rivers, inter-locking canals and river valley gravel pits. The best baits are maggots, pinkies, bloodworms and jokers. These are fished on the surface with a greased line, or with shallow-set pole rigs, at depths down to three feet.

Cloudy groundbait will hold them in numbers. They feed best when rivers and canals are heavily swollen by rain.

BRITISH RECORD
4 oz 4 dr (0.120 kg)

CATFISH

This species has a cult following, but it's a small, dedicated band of anglers, because there aren't that many recognised catfish waters in this country.

Catfish are scavengers and are usually caught on small dead fish although a wide range of baits including squid are used. They will feed in the day, but are more likely to pick up a bait at night.

> **BRITISH RECORD**
> 49 lb 14 oz (22.623 kg).

There are signs that cats are spreading as odd ones have been accidentally caught on southern canals and rivers. On the Continent they reach massive sizes and can exceed 100 lb. A specimen British cat would weigh 20 lb but that's no easy target.

CARP

Intense cultivation of carp has resulted in several varieties but all stem from the fully scaled common or fast growing king carp. These are completely covered in regular sized scales and are frequently streamlined in shape although older specimens might grow very deep. There are two pairs of barbels on the upper lip.

line. To confuse matters still further, it's possible to catch fully scaled mirrors completely covered in large, plate-like scales.

Specimens without any visible scales whatsoever are known as nude or leather carp. You may also hear the term wild carp which in its true form is a fish that has never known any

and canals and feed in open water at all levels, including from the surface. Carp also like overgrown areas and are good at nestling into inaccessible spots. They will often be found in thick weed beds, under lilies and thick cover, even among sunken tree roots.

In the warmer months, carp are very active and feed up in the water, or

Mirror

Leather

Mirrors have an irregular scattering of large scales, notably around the wrist of the tail with odd ones dotted along the back and flanks. There are also linear mirrors with a continuous straight row of scales along the lateral

form of domestication. It is unlikely that these exist in the UK even if you hear fully scaled, torpedo-shaped fish caught from remote, ancient lakes described as wildies.

Carp are widespread in lakes, rivers

actually on the surface. They also patrol the margins and shallows, particularly over gravel bars.

They become more lethargic in winter and may only feed for short periods in deeper water on really cold

DACE

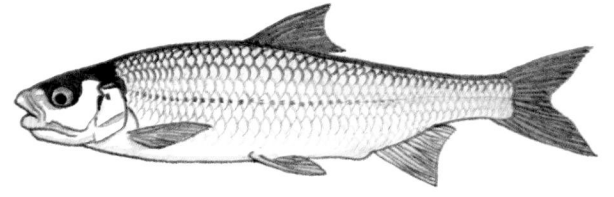

Dace are mainly river and small stream fish, but are also present in some flowing canal venues. They're very active and gather in vast shoals on clear, fast flowing shallows. They will feed at all levels, but are renowned for competing for food up in the water and on the surface.

Dace give bites like greased lightening, so it's quite an achievement to string a catch together. They like maggots, casters, hemp and tares. Sometimes match anglers will fish

---

BRITISH RECORD
1 lb 4 oz 4 dr (0.574 kg).

---

very light rigs for dace and even resort to smaller baits like pinkies to try and put a fair catch together. These silver fish average two to eight ounces on most rivers and sometimes shoal in huge numbers on the shallows. A 1 lb plus dace is an exceptional specimen.

---

days. Carp are a cult fish and many specimen anglers are only interested in this species alone. They will camp out by the waterside for days, even weeks after double-figure fish.

Carp gear is very sophisticated and it's not unusual for the dedicated carp angler to fish with up to three rods resting on special pods and buzzer bars. There's an impressive choice of electronic bite indicators and other assorted gadgetry. In fact, there have been more developments in carp tackle and rigs than in any other area of the sport.

While a static approach, with legered baits is the main line of attack for many carp anglers, these fish will also take floating baits, like bread crust and Chum Mixers. A lot of serious carp men take a stalking rod out with them and leave their main fishing sta-

Crucian

tion from time to time, to wander off in search of cruising, or basking fish.

Luncheon meat, sweetcorn and bread are worth trying for carp, but boilies are now the No.1 bait for this species. These high protein offerings

can be made up to your own recipes and specifications at home, or purchased in exotic flavours, off the shelf in any tackle shop.

Boilies come in many sizes, colours and flavours. There are also countless additives and stimulators which can be applied making them even more potent. Certainly the fish seem to appreciate this new science and appear to be preoccupied with boilies on waters where they are fed in large quantities.

Carp, particularly smaller fish up to 10 lb, will feed on conventional baits like maggots, casters, sweetcorn, bread, hemp and tares. Fish in the 2 lb to 5 lb bracket are heavily stocked in many small lakes and will compete well for these types of feed on light float tackle.

Well stocked stillwaters might also hold ghost carp, which are a cross between commons and kois. These grow up to low double-figures and fight really well for their size.

While many anglers would be pleased with a double-figure com-

mon, mirror, or leather carp, 20 lb is commonly regarded as the barrier to break in specimen fishing circles.

Crucian carp are a smaller relation and rarely exceed 4 lb. These fish are fairly widespread in lakes and canals and prefer small baits like maggots, casters, bread and sweetcorn. Crucians are stocky little fish and are normally a much brighter golden colour than common carp. They are also fully scaled, but are distinguishable from other carp by the lack of barbels on their mouths and their tubby appearance.

This is in complete contrast to the chub-like profile of the grass carp which is now becoming more widespread in the UK. It grazes on all forms of aquatic vegetation and in numerous waters is used as a form of biological weed control, eliminating the need for chemical treatments. But stocking levels are crucial because it is quite capable of completely denuding a fishery of all weed. Like the crucian, it has no barbels and is fully scaled but it is impossible to confuse the two because of the grass carp's wide head and elongated body.

BRITISH CARP RECORDS
51 lb 8 oz (23.358 kg).
Crucian 5 lb 10 oz 8 dr (2.565 kg)
Grass 25 lb 4 oz (11.453 kg).

CHUB

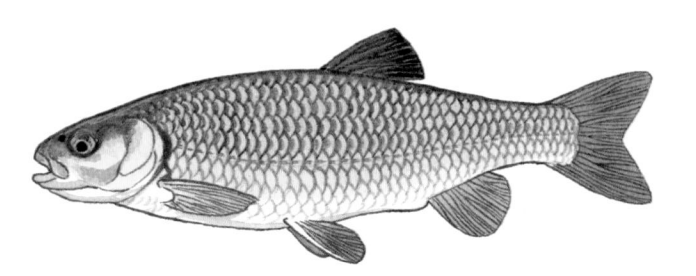

Although chub are primarily a river fish, they do thrive in some canals. Some enormous specimens are also stocked in gravel pits, but they're extremely elusive.

Rivers provide the easiest chances of catching chub. They are a species which has a definite liking for features. If there's overhanging foliage, then it's almost certain a shoal of chub will be in the vicinity – if not tucked right underneath it.

Chub also like streamy water, weir pools, weedy areas and smooth glides – especially if they end in rippling shallows. While it's possible to take good catches in open, flowing water on rivers, canal chub are often more wary and a bait has to be presented very tight to cover to entice a response.

Average sized fish run to 3 lb and often make up good catches on feeder gear. The stick float is a good method in medium flow rates, while the waggler takes over on slower rivers, or when fishing to more distant far bank cover on smaller rivers and canals.

A good quantity of maggots, or casters may be required to keep a shoal of chub interested. They also respond to hemp and tares in summer and autumn.

Larger baits work well for chub. They have a reputation as scavengers, so it's doubtful if they'll ignore anything on the recognised bait lists.

Favourite chub methods are free-lining, link legering, or trotting with large capacity floats, often called chubbers. Big baits like luncheon meat, bread and lobworms are popular. Other good chub baits are slugs, waspgrub, crayfish, small dead fish and sweetcorn. They will even take spinners meant for perch and pike.

Chub feed year round, even in very cold temperatures when other species lay low. A specimen sized chub is usually over 4 lb.

> **BRITISH RECORD**
> 8 lb 4 oz (3.743 kg).

GRAYLING

These handsome river fish are easy to recognise, due to their large, sail-like dorsal fins. They are members of the salmon family and have an adipose fin with large black spots on the flanks.

Grayling are shoal fish and prefer clean, fast flowing water and thrive in smaller salmon rivers. These fish are streamlined and even small specimens fight hard. When released, they must be held head first into the current to recover their strength otherwise they could float away belly up.

The best method is long trotting with baits like maggots using all-balsa, or Avon style floats. A 2 lb grayling is very good – over 3 lb is a specimen.

> **BRITISH RECORD**
> 4 lb 3 oz (1.899 kg)

GUDGEON

Gudgeon are bottom feeders, common in rivers, canals and some lakes. These very small fish look similar to barbel and tend to hug the margins to avoid the attention of predators.

They weigh no more than a few ounces and matchmen are the only anglers who might fish for them seriously when low weights are expected on poor canal or river venues.

Gudgeon are shoal fish, so some surprising weights of them can be achieved. A busy competitive angler might catch several hundred on a short pole rig. Canal catches can reach 10 lb over five hours. On some rivers up to 20 lb of gudgeon is possible.

Best baits are maggots, pinkies, squatts, bloodworms and jokers.

> **BRITISH RECORD**
> 5 oz (0.141 kg).

Eel

Eels are migratory fish and small ones, or bootlaces as anglers often call them, can be a nuisance on rivers. Great mystery surrounds the life cycle of the eel. They mature at varying ages, but usually after around nine years in freshwater, and then make their amazing journey downstream and across the Atlantic Ocean to the spawning grounds in the Sargasso Sea off the Bahamas. They spawn and die with each female releasing several million eggs.

Exactly how these hatch and find their way back across the Atlantic isn't fully known but many millions of elvers eventually return to our river systems and spread out into all kinds of waters.

Specimen sized fish of over 3 lb are mainly found in gravel pits and lakes where they'll often leave the bottom to feed in mid-water or even higher.

They tear at their food, are very long-lived (possibly as long as 50 years) and become considerably less active in winter.

Small eels readily snap up maggots, casters and worms. Big eels tend to become mainly worm or fish feeders and this distinction is quite marked in some waters.

> **BRITISH RECORD**
> 11 lb 2 oz (5.046 kg).

Perch

Small perch are often the first fish a novice angler catches. When they are only a few ounces in size, these fish show little caution and willingly take poorly presented hook baits.

Perch are predators and like a mobile bait. Top anglers respond to that by deliberately making their tackle behave erratically, twitching and lifting maggot and worm baits, to try and catch a bonus perch, or two.

Perch are found in most types of fishery. Up to 2 lb in size they take maggots, pinkies, casters and all types of worm., Specimen sized fish can be caught on spinners, lobworms and some small livebaits, like gudgeon and minnows.

Because of their predatory instincts, these distinctive striped fish, with their prominent, spiny dorsal fins, tend to be found near features which afford cover for small fry. You can expect to find perch alongside weedbeds, margins, ledges, overhanging cover, reeds, pilings and bridges. They often give away their presence by scattering small fry.

Perch are shoal fish for most of their lives, but larger specimens over 2 lb can drift off into pairs, or become loners.

Small perch usually give a response throughout the season, larger stillwater fish become more active in autumn and winter.

> **BRITISH RECORD**
> 5 lb 9 oz (2.523 kg).

Ruffe

When fishing canals and some rivers you may catch a fish with an identical outline to the perch, but with spotted instead of striped flanks. This is the ruffe, a bottom feeding member of the

> **BRITISH RECORD**
> 5 oz 4 dr (0.148 kg).

perch family which only grows to around 15cm in length.

Unlike perch, the first and second dorsal fins on the ruffe are joined. They eagerly accept maggots and worms. Sometimes you'll get a response from ruffe when no other species is feeding.

PIKE

Pike are the most impressive predators in freshwater and sit on top of the food chain. Their large, wide mouths hide rows of razor sharp teeth which are inward pointing. Prey are swallowed head first and rarely escape.

Their streamlined bodies are also geared for catching prey fish. Pike tend to lay up in ambush until potential food swims close and then accelerate into the attack at amazing speed.

They are vital in balancing stocks in most mixed fisheries and will often pick off injured, poorly or dead fish.

Pike are never far away from features like overhanging trees and bushes, weed and rush beds, underwater bars, inlets, outlets and islands.

Livebaiting is a deadly way of catching them but the method is banned on some fisheries to protect the image of the sport or as a disease deterrent to eliminate free movement of bait fish between different waters.

Dead coarse fish will catch a lot of pike, but sea fish like herrings, sprats, smelt, mackerel and sardines are usually far more productive. Pike can be caught on float tackle, or legered baits. The latter are often fished with electronic bite indicators, similar to those used by carp anglers.

Another very exciting method of taking these fish is with spinner baits, or plugs. There's a massive range of these types of lures to choose from. A double-figure pike is a good fish, a 20-pounder is an exceptional specimen.

> **BRITISH RECORD**
> 46 lb 13 oz (21.234 kg).

ROACH

Roach are the most popular and widely distributed British coarse fish. You will have to be quick with small ones and extremely skilful to tempt older, wiser fish over the 1 lb mark.

This species takes on a slightly different appearance depending on habitat. Roach from coloured canal and lake fisheries are rather pale, with virtually a bleached look about them. But the same species from a clear, small river can positively glow with colour. There's no mistaking the bright red fins of a clean river fish.

Lake roach rarely keep to set boundaries. In the warm months they will rise up in the water to regular feed, even boil on the surface. They

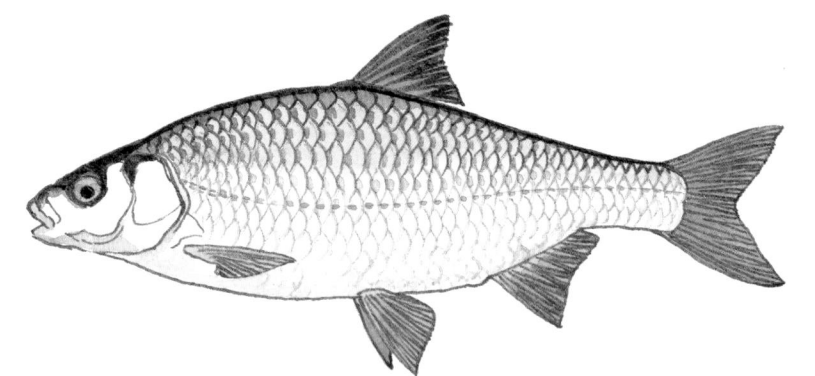

tend to revert to bottom feeding in winter, but clever feeding will still activate them into competing up in the water.

Canal roach are very canny. Very delicate lines, tiny hooks and small baits are required here. Squatts, hemp, punched bread, bloodworm...all have special roaching techniques built up around them.

River roach will respond to conventional maggot and caster baits, hemp, tares and wheat, but again they need to be fed and fished for with great care and more than a smidgen of skill. Big river roach also show a liking for seed baits and larger bread offerings. A 1 lb roach is a good fish while a two-pounder represents a magical milestone.

> **BRITISH RECORD**
> 4 lb 3 oz (1.899 kg).

HYBRIDS

On heavily stocked waters, species like roach and bream often spawn in the same areas. This can result in cross-fertilisation of eggs and sometimes produces hybrids.

Roach-bream hybrids tend to have the body shape of bream, but smaller, silvery scales (rather than large bronze ones,) on the upper flanks of their bodies. This usually signifies their roach ancestry.

Some hybrids are more roach shaped and lighter coloured. This can fool anglers into thinking they have caught a specimen roach! The tell tale sign, which usually gives the game away, is the anal fin, which is concave and much longer than that of a true roach.

These are very good sporting fish and can grow up to 4 lb in size on many waters. This type of hybrid can be very active and will fall to most methods.

RUDD

Surface feeding rudd are found in lakes, but also canals and rivers.

Rudd are sometimes mistaken for roach, but the bottom lip on rudd protrudes beyond the top one. Rudd's fins are also more crimson than red.

These fish are located in reedy bays and close to weed cover. They also like overhanging foliage, but will just as readily drift out into open water, particularly if a ripple is carrying insect life across a lake.

Rudd compete vigorously on the surface for maggots, casters, hemp and bread in summer. They can be caught on greased line surface rigs, or small wagglers with little shot positioned down the line. Regular loose feed and soft, cloudy groundbait is often needed to keep them interested.

They vanish after the first frosts and don't reappear until the summer. A 2 lb fish is regarded as a specimen.

BRITISH RECORD
4 lb 8 oz (2.041 kg).

STICKLEBACKS AND MINNOWS

Stickleback

Minnow

Only the most desperate of match anglers might actually have a go at fishing for these tiddlers! The common three-spined stickleback is found everywhere from drainage ditches to estuary waters but is a pest because of its ability to destroy baits. They peck at maggots until you're left with an empty skin and sometimes get the bait firmly lodged down their red throats.

Minnows are a nuisance during low summer flows on rivers and sometimes it's very difficult to get through them with maggot baits.

BRITISH RECORD
minnow 13 dr (0.023 kg).

ZANDER

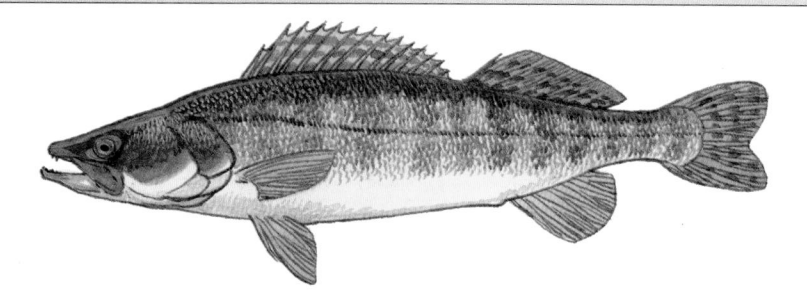

Zander, or pike-perch as they are sometimes called, were first imported in the late 19th century when they were released into ponds at Woburn Abbey in Bedfordshire. But the most significant stocking was in the Great Ouse Relief Channel – a supposedly safe base from which they have subsequently spread far and wide.

They bred very successfully in the slow, deep and coloured waters of the Channel and proved such active predators that they caused a crash in the populations of prey species. There have been similar reports from canals in the Midlands where zander were illegally stocked.

But nature now appears to have achieved a reasonable balance.

BRITISH RECORD
18 lb 10 oz (8.448 kg).

Tench

Odd tench to 4 lb are taken in slack bays or backwaters on major rivers. Many canals also contain prolific stocks of tench and they are sometimes recorded up to 7 lb from these venues. But really big tench are more associated with lakes and reservoirs where they can reach double-figures.

Best fishing times for tench are in the early morning and late evening. They are caught in large numbers in the summer, then tend to fade until the back-end of the season. Odd fish may be caught through the winter but they are not predictable at this time of the year.

Tench are margin feeders, but also like weedy areas and bars on the edge of deep water. They will often forage into very shallow water and backwaters in warm weather.

Although noted as bottom feeders, tench will compete up in the water with regular feeding and have also been known to take surface baits like bread crust.

On carp venues they frequently become pre-occupied with boilies. They will take maggots (reds are a favourite), worms, casters, sweetcorn, bread baits and luncheon meat.

Float fishing, legering and feeder tactics all work well on their day for this species. You will often know when a tench is rooting about on the bottom, by the clusters of small bubbles it sends fizzing to the surface. A specimen tench would be over 7 lb on most waters.

BRITISH RECORD
14 lb 7 oz (6.548 kg).

Unhooking And Handling Code

Below: **Repeat captures of the same fish are common and it's every angler's responsibility to handle and return his fish to the water as carefully and quickly as possible. Hold larger specimens in the wet mesh of the landing net, taking care to avoid exerting pressure on the gills. Use a suitable sized disgorger if the hook lies deeper inside the mouth.**

Below: **Forceps are an efficient tool for removing bigger hooks from specimen fish. Unhooking mats are essential if you intend taking up carp or pike fishing and they must be wet before use. But never lay any fish on hard ground, no matter what its size.**

Right: Zero in a wet weigh sling on the scales before recording an exceptional fish. You can also use a strong plastic bag for the smaller specimens. But suspend the fish over a grassy bank or water in case of mishap. The same applies when photographing a fish – it should be held low to the ground over an unhooking mat or grass at the water's edge.

● Barbel frequently fight to the point of exhaustion. Return them in that condition and they could float away belly-up. They must be held head-first into the flow until they recover. Alternatively, stake them out in the stream using a special tube made of soft material.

Right below: Ideally, fish should be returned to the water immediately with the minimal amount of handling. That's the basic code. But if you must use a keepnet, stake it out in deep water, giving the fish maximum free- dom inside. At the end of the session, do not withdraw the net completely from the water and carry it up the bank. That could result in fish losing scales as they tumble down the whole length of the net and thrash about in the base. Far better to release them in the water as demonstrated here. Lift the end of the net and guide the fish through the mouth.

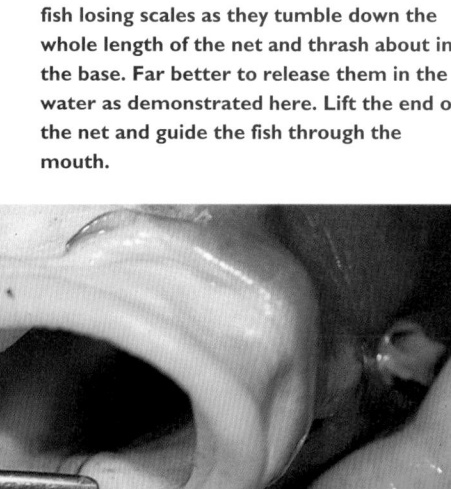

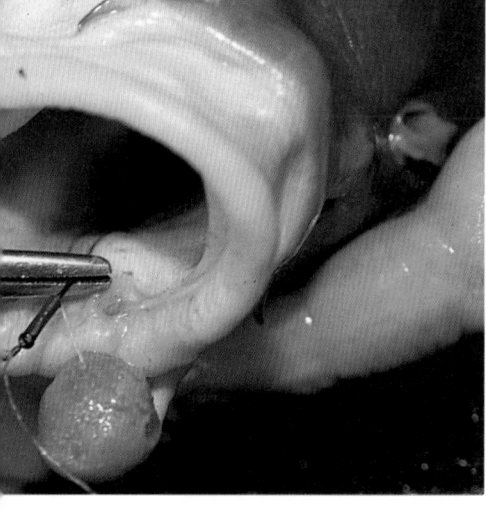

RIVER FISHING

The golden rule when fishing flowing water is to feed the swim very regularly. It's essential because river fish soon drift away unless you're in a swim where the shoals are held captive by a pronounced feature.

As with any venue, features are an important guide in locating river fish. Productive areas usually include stretches of bank with overhanging foliage, slacks, lock cuttings, reed beds, weirs, islands and bends. The confluence with a tributary is also worthy of investigation.

But on running water it's possible to draw fish wherever you are fishing by clever feeding. Many river species are nomadic and they soon locate your feed – as long as it's fed regularly in the right quantity to make the fish compete for it.

More subtle features like clear runs between weed beds may have to be pinpointed with the aid of a good pair of Polaroid sunglasses. These eradicate reflective glare and make it a lot easier to see beneath the surface.

Regular feeding draws fish out from the weed. It may take some time, but it's often possible to keep on building this type of swim until a really good catch accumulates.

Steady runs above broken, shallow water might also hold many fish. Some of your feed will filter down into the rapids and draw others up. It's also well worth remembering that fish like variations in flow, so look carefully at swims with a crease line, where faster water abuts a steady run.

Water at the tail-end of weir run-offs is always well oxygenated and usually holds plenty of fish. And big shoals frequently hide up right beneath moored boats, particularly when the craft are tied up on the quieter, far bank.

Don't get downhearted if the only vacant swims on a river venue are straight and feature-less. Sport may not be instantaneous but a

A successful strike at long range – but with regular feeding it's possible to draw the shoal upriver.

patient, well thought out approach often results in some really good catches by the end of the day.

Shallows are often ignored but these, too, might hold substantial shoals. The fishing can be surprisingly easy once you've sorted out a suitable rig. These pacey swims usually produce more positive bites.

Two Lines of Attack

Feature swims like islands and overhanging cover often have fish laying tight to them, but it's not wise to dive straight into these areas with your tackle. One false move, such as a bad cast, or a lost fish could ruin your chances for the rest of the day.

There are two good ways of working at these types of swim. A proven match technique is to feed the feature regularly for an hour or so and in the meantime fish another part of the swim. The idea is to get the fish taking baits confidently, so when you do go out with your tackle, competing fish will be less prone to spook when you catch one or two of them.

It doesn't matter if you spend this initial period whipping out some small fish on the pole, or on a close-in running line rig. The trick is to keep yourself occupied, while still remembering to regularly feed the area which will eventually become your main line of attack.

The second method entails trying to feed fish just a little bit away from the feature, in the hope that you can take odd ones at the edge of the shoal. If this works you may be able to stall fishing tight to the feature until much later in the session. This may well be the best route to choose

Seasonal Factors

Fish are more active in summer and autumn when they often show a preference for shallow, streamy water. But following the first night frosts, rivers begin to change and so do the feeding habits of the fish. They become more lethargic and are less inclined to chase after baits with the same enthusiasm they showed in the warmer weather.

Large shoals may move into deeper, less pacey water, in preparation for the winter floods. These fish will require a totally different approach.

In warmer weather, a swim develops in many ways depending on how the fish react to your feeding. You'll obviously get through a lot more bait chasing a shoal around the swim, particularly if the fish move up in the water. You may also have to feed lots anyway, in order to get through the small fish which intercept a great deal of bait before it has a chance to reach the bottom.

In winter this isn't such a problem and you may be able to feed much less, in the knowledge that it's reaching bottom. That is not to say regular feeding has to be ignored. It's probably even more important, because you are going to have to work even harder in coaxing lethargic fish into showing interest.

During the early months of the season, baits fished up in the water and trotted at the pace of the current will take good catches. But as feed requirements drop, techniques must often change too. You will have to learn to slow the tackle down to coax bites when the going is hard. Stick float rigs may have to be edged through the swim at half pace, leger tackle and the feeder become more important methods because static baits might possibly pull more bites.

Some feature pegs remain good all-year round, but others are seasonal, so you will have to try to learn to read the river. This also means that certain swims which appeared virtually devoid of fish earlier in the year, might be well worth investigating later in the season.

Extra water in the river totally changes its character yet again. Slacker water which teemed with minnows and small fry in the summer, often holds big fish now. They may also only be a few feet out from the bank. When the river's up and coloured like this, it's even possible to catch fish in the slacks provided by drainage ditches and cattle drinks. It's not unusual for the fish to forage up onto areas which were dry land before the river rose.

Apart from varying bait requirements with the changing seasons, tackle

if feeder tackle is the only way to reach the fish.

It is very tempting to go for a couple of good fish quickly, but if you fish tight to features at the start of a session, this is all you are likely to take! The two methods described are more reliable for doubling, or even trebling the catch potentials.

FEEDING TRICKS

With less obvious features you will have to use your imagination a little more. The fish could be shoaled anywhere on a long run between weed, or along a slow sweeping bend in the river. But instead of feeding solely where your float is going in, begin the session by putting some feed right down the swim and then at five yard intervals back to where you are positioned. That way, some of the free offerings are bound to be found

quicker. Only do this once, then revert to feeding regularly at the head of the swim. It's a good opening gambit because the fish will move up to you a lot faster than they would with just the one feed area.

In seemingly featureless swims, try a couple of exploratory casts before starting to feed. As you search the run with your tackle you may discover underwater weedbeds, or a very pronounced inside ledge. This helps to decide the most suitable line of attack.

Similarly, there may be areas of the swim where it's too snaggy to run your tackle through at full depth. It's better to discover where these are before loose feeding the fish into areas where you can't catch them.

There's also little tricks you can employ on totally featureless parts of the river. In order to

Left: Summer fishing generally produces more bites simply because the fish are more active.

Right: Hampshire Avon specialist Bob James draws a chub over the net after a spirited fight in the shallows.

modifications should also be considered carefully. When the fish are feeding well in summer and autumn, you might get away with a double hookbait, impaled on a size 16 hook tied to 1.7 lb line. The same end tackle on a cold, clear river might not catch you anything! You may have to scale down to a single maggot bait, fished on a 20 hook and 1 lb bottom to tempt a response.

But remember, with the fish being more lethargic, you will have a much better chance of landing bigger samples on fragile tackle. You still have to take care to balance the rig, but if you take it easy you may well be surprised by what you can land.

get the best from these spots, the fish will probably have to be drawn a fair distance. On faster flowing waters, some bait will naturally filter downstream and pull fish up over long periods of continuous feeding. But on medium and slow paced waters this won't be the case. Baits like maggots and casters will sink to the bottom only a few yards downstream of where they have been fed and are likely to stay there.

Another match fishing technique is to feed big maggots at the head of these swims, but also to feed smaller maggots like pinkies at the tail-end of the trot. These take twice as long to settle and will eventually pull bonus fish onto your main line where the big maggots are being fed.

If a river swim is wide enough, it might pay to vary your attack between, say, a stick float line and a further waggler swim. If one method dries up, you have somewhere to go with the other and can rest the first part of the swim, which may come back strongly – if you keep a little feed going in while it's rested.

IT'S CRITICAL TO PERMUTATE BAITS

For the first few weeks of a new season, rivers respond well to a bait like maggots, fed quite heavily. You may need quite a few pints to draw fish and feed off small fry and surface feeders like hungry bleak and small dace. If the water receives heavy angling pressure, the fish population soon wises up to this approach and a change bait like casters, or even hempseed might bring better results.

When fish are taking maggots avidly, bottom rigs will probably catch early in the day, then you

will have to change to strung shotting, or even a light, long pole rig. The waggler is also very effective in this instance.

The best way to catch competing fish up in the water is to feed first, then drop the tackle in over the top. This gets the hookbait falling in unison with the free offerings and brings more positive bites. By feeding every cast in this way, a lot of bait will obviously get used up.

Casters are more effective for bigger fish and when these are catching well you probably won't need so many. Caster tends to be a better bottom bait on rivers. Some of the feed will still be lost to small fish, of course, but in summer this bait works particularly well with hempseed and holds fish in the swim.

If you can catch good fish tripping the bottom with caster, you might find it's better to feed these less regularly, say every three or four casts. More casters will avoid the smaller fish this way and you can still continue feeding hemp, in-between times.

If there are a lot of roach and dace around, it's always worth trying hemp on the hook. This has a tendency to work better later in a session and you can stop feeding casters altogether if the seed brings regular bites. If you can't connect with the hemp bites, a tare should produce more hittable responses, even if these haven't been fed. The other advantage of using this slightly larger hookbait is that it doesn't come off the hook as easily as hemp, so you can strike several times without having to re-bait.

Hemp works better as a feed with maggots later in the year. It's still a good holding bait and won't fill the fish up too quickly. In a typical winter swim, it's often possible to build a good weight by feeding a dozen grains of hemp and just three or four maggots every cast.

Loose feeding is likely to out-score groundbait at river venues on nine out of ten outings. But it's worth carrying some groundbait for these odd occasions. A heavy groundbait is useful in deeper swims, for getting a mixture of hemp and casters down quickly, especially if you are fishing the pole. After a while, the fish get used to a small ball of feed going in regularly. If this seems to unsettle them, another trick is to feed several large balls to get a fair bit of bait down, then to top up very occasionally during periods when bites have tailed off.

Softer groundbait also revives shallower swims, when fishing for species like dace, roach and chub. Fish are inquisitive creatures and cloud groundbait simulates the bottom being

Try hemp on the hook when there's a lot of roach in the swim.

stirred up. They associate this happening with food, so the odd ball of groundbait can work wonders for a flagging swim.

Blockend feeders can be fished with neat maggots, or on really long sessions it's possible to make this expensive bait go much further by half filling the feeder with hemp first, before adding the maggots.

As mentioned earlier, when casting a long way, you'll also save on wastage by covering the lower exit holes on feeders with waterproof, electrical tape. This stops bait wriggling out while you line up the rig and while it's airborne.

Groundbait feeders are more economical. A pint of casters, a pint of hemp and a smattering of pinkies and squatts go a long way in half a kilo of groundbait. It's best to introduce several baits like this because, apart from letting you experiment with hookbaits, a good mixture of offerings pulls a wide variety of species into the swim.

CALCULATING THE BAIT MENU

There's a big difference in bait requirements if you intend to follow a roving approach instead of staying put in the same swim. Some anglers like to travel light and drop big hookbaits like luncheon meat, or bread, into likely looking spots, giving each swim just a couple of casts, before moving on. This approach does bring results by the law of averages, simply because the chances are the bait is going to be dropped right on the nose of a good fish.

Half a loaf of fresh bread and a tin of luncheon meat may be sufficient for a day's fishing this way.

The stationary approach favoured by most river anglers will invariably require more specialist bait menus. And these will vary with the changing seasons:

MAGGOTS In the warmer months, it may be necessary to spray the swim with several pints of maggots, to work your way through small fish, or draw big fish away from cover. A stick float session would need at least two pints, a waggler approach 4-6 pints and possibly up to a gallon if big feeders are being used for species like chub and barbel.

In winter, it's possible to halve these quantities, perhaps supplementing loose fed maggots with more hemp.

Barbel like this seven-pounder captured by TV wildlife cameraman Hugh Miles demand a lot of bait to get them preoccupied and overcome their natural caution.

CASTERS Two pints of casters should be adequate for a long summer stick float session. Between three and four pints could be used on a waggler line, but this is halved if you intend to feed hemp as well. Two pints of this bait will satisfy most groundbait feeder requirements. In winter, a pint of casters goes a long way. There's rarely a need for more than two pints, even if you intend switching between the float and a groundbait feeder.

HEMP Still a relatively cheap feed bait and it's a good idea to always have a little more than you think you will need, just in case a good day depletes other bait stocks rather too quickly. Hemp teams well with both maggots and casters. Two pints is normally sufficient for most methods, unless the target species is barbel, where it can be very effective to feed 4-6 pints of the seeds to form a good carpet on the bottom.

TARES A handful of tares is all you will need for hookbaits when fishing with hemp. There are odd occasions when a pint of these larger seeds will pay dividends when chub are the target on long range waggler tackle. You don't need to feed a lot of tares, but they do out-distance hempseed by some 15-20 metres, if the fish won't move in.

BREAD A good winter bait on rivers. Flake and crust work well on a straight leger, or in combination with crumb feed in an open-end feeder. Half of an uncut loaf should be enough for a session, with perhaps the other half of the loaf being liquidised for feed. This can be bound together with a couple of pints of breadcrumb groundbait. Punched bread is also good for big roach and chub on float gear. Take several thick slices of white bread for the hook, together with 3–4 pints of liquidised bread, or punch crumb as groundbait.

WORMS A pot of redworms is a useful standby bait when rivers are carrying extra water. On a link leger, or laid-on over-depth, this bait pulls bonus chub, perch and big roach. It's a good option to try when fishing the open-end feeder. Lobworms are worth experimenting with when roving the banks for chub and barbel or legering in known big fish areas.

PINKIES When the river is out of form, a pint of pinkies helps pull fish, if fed down the swim. They are also a good scratching bait in winter. A few fed into open-end feeder mixes can also be worthwhile. Pinkies are sometimes used in flood conditions to take big bleak catches by fishing up in the water in slacks.

Everything tastes good to a chub including stewing steak.

Rig Strategies

Where possible, keep float rigs versatile. This allows you to modify the tackle quickly if the fish follow expected feeding trends and move up in the water, as good feeding technique begins to take effect.

More small shot positioned down the rig, instead of far fewer larger ones, opens up greater possibilities here. It's well worth the time and trouble to group several No.8 shot as a bulk on waggler tackle for instance, if you know that later in the session it will only take a few seconds to spread them out, to form a better on-the-drop rig.

The same thinking applies to top and bottom attached floats, bulks can be split up more effectively if they're formed with smaller shot.

If you start fishing a stick with strung shot, and the float set at depth, there are several different ways this rig can be developed, to suit the changing demands of the swim. You can deepen off the tackle and hold it back slightly, to try and gain extra bites. If the float begins to ride up as you tighten the line to it, try adding an extra shot, something like a No.8, below the float. This will dot it back down as you trot the tackle downstream on a tight line and keep the float leaning backwards.

If this rig still seems to be moving through the swim too quickly, group the smaller strung shot together, so that they form a bulk, a couple of feet away from the hook. This normally stabilises a rig better when trying to slow it against the flow.

Similar shot movements are beneficial with waggler tackle. You start a waggler session with a bulk of No.8 shot set three feet from the hook and a couple of No.10 dropper shot spread below this. Initially, this helps get the bait through the small fish which are always active as you begin a feeding campaign.

But later, as the swim develops, there's quite a good chance that some of the bigger fish will scare off the small fry, so you will be able to spread the bulk well out, to catch competing fish up in the water. If you find that there are too many shot down the line for this, a few can be pushed right up under the float's locking shot.

Waggler bulks of small shot can also be spread down the lower half of the rig, at shorter intervals, to act as a brake if you wish to try dragging the tackle over-depth.

It's not possible to be so versatile with specialised float designs like chubbers. But bulk weights on Avons and balsas can be spread out slightly in deeper water. This helps pull these floats through better, if there's an undertow.

Occasionally, downstream wind makes it tricky fishing a top and bottom attached float. If the line bows out, to the side of the float, pulling it off course, a back shot solves the problem. First, try a No.10, positioned two feet above the float. If this doesn't work, use a No.8 which should definitely provide enough weight to keep the line properly mended behind the float.

Waggler tackle can also be back shotted, providing you are using a floating line.

As you progress in fishing, you will get to know the type of swims which need a dual approach. A top and bottom fixed float may be discarded for a waggler rig, fished over the same line, if fish move up.

Once you are proficient with bigger stick float rigs, you might want to experiment trying one over a redundant waggler line, if it is within casting range. It's surprising the difference a slower bait presentation makes in these cases.

Very shallow river swims are normally best approached with waggler tackle. There's a special, short bodied waggler called a Trent Trotter which works well down to minimal depths of just six inches.

When using feeder tackle on flowing water, always try and point the rod downstream in its rests.

Balance just enough weight on the feeder to hold bottom and feed a little line out when the rod is set in this way, bites will then be more positive. This is called fishing the bow, simply because the force of the current puts a bow in the line.

A taking fish will upset this delicate balance and normally result in the quivertip dropping back as the feeder moves. The pressure of the current on the line is normally enough to set the hook, otherwise you gently lean the rod into the fish. This is a far more productive method than tight lining to the feeder.

Squatts Only take a pint of these on river venues if you know the open-end feeder offers chances of finding skimmers and bream.

Meats, Pastes and Cheeses These are only normally used on the hook. A small tin of luncheon meat, or a ball of bread or cheese paste about the size of an orange, is usually sufficient for a river trip.

Chub anglers have recently discovered stewing steak and minced beef are effective big river baits. About 4 oz of steak suffices as hookbait and a pound of mince is separated and bulked out with several pints of breadcrumb. This method is worth trying on float, or feeder tackle.

Groundbait It's not a bad idea to carry a bag of heavy consistency, Continental groundbait for deeper river swims or for use with the open-end feeder. Crushed hemp is a good binder and attracting agent if you know the open-end feeder succeeds with chub on the water in question. A few pints of breadcrumb are useful for bread sessions in winter.

PIT AND LAKE FISHING

GRAVEL PITS

Some of these waters display the clarity of tap water, while others which contain dense stocks of bream and carp are an impenetrable soup of disturbed bottom sediment. Clear, shallow water usually encourages heavy weed growth. Species like tench, perch, roach, pike and carp will always be close to well weeded areas.

Many gravel pits are dotted with tree covered islands. Large shoals of carp and bream congregate alongside these features.

Gravel extraction leaves troughs and ridges. In summer and autumn, many fish will be found feeding on the shallow, gravel bars, or patrolling the shelves running into deeper water.

Unlike many stillwaters, the deepest water on a lot of gravel pits is often around the margins where channels have been formed for barges to haul the gravel away. These gulleys can accumu-

late a lot of natural food and they will nearly always hold a large head of fish like roach, perch, tench and skimmers.

Weather conditions influence the movement of gravel pit shoals. Many anglers make the mistake of heading for sheltered areas, when the banks facing into the wind have coloured water close in, caused by the wave action. This disturbs a lot of natural food and is normally a signal that big bream, tench and carp catches are a distinct possibility.

In very clear pits, a fish holding feature greatly enhances your chances. The type of swims worth investigating might have one, or more features such as tree or weed cover, islands, rush lined bays, visible gravel bars and dark water gulleys.

On an open swim with no such pointers, it's a fair bet the best chances of catching any fish will be long range leger, feeder, or waggler tactics.

Lakes

Large lily beds are a welcome feature on clear water lakes as they provide abundant food and shelter beneath the canopy. Many of the characteristics which make for special swims on pits also apply. Deeper water close in is worth investigating, but on bright days long range tactics are important.

Coloured lakes are normally quite shallow and very productive during the warmer months. It's not so vital to seek out feature pegs for a big

There's a gully running close to the bank and that's where Dave Coster hooked this sizeable bream.

catch on these waters, although good features will still hold fish.

Small, day ticket lakes with artificially high stock densities have become much more widespread. It's possible to achieve good catches from most swims in the inevitably coloured water. An attacking feeding policy may prove more important than swim selection.

TACTICS FOR A BIG CATCH

As with river fisheries, it's not always a good idea to be too quick off the mark in trying to exploit a feature. Many stillwaters respond quite well to close-in tactics at the start of a session, particu-

larly at first light. Fish tend to feed in the margins at night and some linger on into the first hours of daylight.

If the swim has a distant feature it's a good idea to feed this up for an hour or so, while first trying to take some fish from a nearer line. When starting close-in, more time needs to be spent plumbing the depth than you might allot to a river swim. Bottom terrain is an important pointer on stillwaters as to where most fish will be caught. Lake fish have more time to inspect a bait and tend to feed more confidently on ledges, or close to weed cover.

Drawing fish with feed is a slower process when there is no flow. Instead, the bait must be

HOW SPORT FLUCTUATES

Pits and lakes are normally most prolific during the warmer months. Sport slows dramatically in really cold weather unless you are after pike, which become very active in clear, cold water. Many stillwaters pick up at the back-end of the season, as temperatures rise with

the March winds and fish shoal up, in preparation for spawning.

In summer, pit and lake fish may vacate deep water and actively search for food in the shallows and at medium depths. Many species are also prone to feeding up in the water as they compete for feed.

A fair amount of feed is needed at these periods and there are also some

seasonal baits well worth considering.

It's unwise to totally ignore stillwaters in winter. The fish must still feed, but need much less, as they are less active. They tend to switch on for shorter periods, usually when daytime temperatures reach their peak, or during the last hour of daylight. Certainly little bait is required in cold weather.

It's possible to use heavier tackle in

presented in areas where the fish patrol, or live, or feel safe.

Once you have gained a good mental picture of the swim at close range, by spending several minutes with a plummet, you may begin fishing near a weed bed, or just over a nearside ledge. It can pay to simply loose feed maggots, or casters. Fish are often resident by such features and this tactic won't scare them.

Groundbait is much more important in still-waters to get a swim going. But it should never be introduced blindly, because it will still spook fish if it's thrown directly over them.

Initial loose feeding might take a couple of quick fish, then bites cease. Now is the time to kick-start the swim with some groundbait. A couple of balls of fine cloud mix is one option. This will leave a fine carpet of particles on the bottom. A regular ball every five minutes or so will probably activate small fish into feeding up in the water. This approach is developed gradually with loose feed, into attracting larger fish later on in the day. Or you may wish to adopt a big fish approach from the off, by using a slightly heavier groundbait mix, putting in several balls, well laced with hemp and casters.

Groundbait attracts fish on its own, but a lot of the time it works better in unison with loose feed, or as a carrier for loose feed. On hard fished waters, the more cautious larger fish are likely to

Right: This mirror carp fell to a grain of sweetcorn fished just off the bottom.

Left: Coloured water makes it possible to use heavier tackle and you'll need it for powerful specimens like this tench.

warmer, coloured water and may be essential if good fish like tench and carp are active. It's not unusual to use 1.5 lb to 2.5 lb hooklengths on the waggler and feeder during the warmer months. But as with river fishing, colder, clearer water often warrants lighter gear and lighter gauge hooks to tempt bites.

In summer, larger hooks are disguised by bigger baits. Double helpings of maggots and casters sort out bigger fish from the fry.

Sweetcorn is effective for tench, bream and carp. Fruit flavoured boilies are also very good. Seed baits like hemp and tares are worth trying, particularly if you are having small fish trouble.

Smaller offerings go hand in hand with smaller hooks in winter. This applies if you are looking for a catch of fish, rather than odd bigger fish.

Big baits like boilies are still worth persevering with for species like carp on specimen gear. Sweetcorn tends to lose its effectiveness but bread baits are always possible winners.

Bottom baits are much the best in winter, although a surface bait might tempt the odd good fish on some of the milder days. Fish will feed at all levels in warmer weather.

In clearer, frost affected water, cloudy groundbait and small pieces of punched bread might spark a response. Baits like squatts, bloodworm and pinkies activate smaller fish and possibly provoke later interest from larger species. It's more a waiting game with bigger baits.

lay just off a groundbaited area, so spray some loose feed just beyond the main line of attack.

It may be possible to keep an inside line producing bites for a fair time, or at least until the sun gets up. But unless you are fishing a particularly well stocked water, once this area fades, it normally stays dead until the evening.

This is why it's such a good idea to prebait a more distant swim for later in the session. If it's a feature you've been feeding, approach this in the same way as on a river. Take as many fish as possible by dropping your tackle short, before attempting to fish tighter in.

Open water swims are also worth prebaiting for later in the day. You might discover a ledge further out with your waggler tackle, or need to search at even greater distances with a bomb.

To do this, tie a reasonably weighty Arlesey bomb on the reel line of a quivertip rod. If you count the bomb down on each cast, until the quivertip drops back, allowing one foot per second, you'll obtain a rough idea of the depth. Working this way and by casting around the swim, any underwater ledges and shelves should soon become apparent. Feed these features with several balls of groundbait, well laced with free offerings like casters, hemp and squatts. You can leave fish to settle over this, while you start on an inside line. Later on you can try leger, or open-end feeder tackle over the prebaited area.

There's no need for top and bottom attached floats on stillwaters, except on the pole, which is discussed in Chapter 10. On running line, main lake methods are waggler, open-end feeder and bomb. The maggot feeder also has limited applications, particularly on small carp waters.

The waggler is normally fished at full depth to begin with, but in the warmer months the fish can move up in the water. When this happens, an attacking approach, feeding lots of loose feed, or groundbait, or a combination of both, can bring some big catches on more shallow set waggler rigs.

Feeding

It's difficult to predict how different venues might respond to groundbait. Sometimes quite a lot needs introducing before the swim switches on. Certainly, putting a fair amount out is a good bet on a second line of attack, if it's left to settle for a long period.

Normally when fishing within float range, just a couple of light balls of cloud gets the swim going. You could prolong things with loose feed after that, or add groundbait occasionally to hold the fish. It's a case of feeling your way.

When after species like tench and bream, you must consider gambling on initial heavy feeding, otherwise nearby anglers might feed your fish into their swims. If you are fishing a long way from others, this may not be a worry. But certainly if you do fill in one part of the swim, it's vital to keep another area lightly fed, so your day isn't a total disaster if things go wrong.

Generally speaking, moderate groundbait and regular loose feed brings a good response on many coloured stillwaters. But on clearer venues, you may need to keep busy with cloudy groundbait to activate and draw the fish. It will probably also be necessary to fish at long range with a soft groundbait mix carrying squatts and casters. A groundbait catapult is clearly a must. A soft mix, long hooklength and open-end feeder rig are good in this situation.

When there's a lot of small carp in a water, regular soft groundbait and some floating casters, or maggots will get the fish boiling on top.

Groundbaiting may not be so effective in winter and could even be the kiss of death on some venues. It's best to be ultra careful and precise with its use in cold weather. Only try the odd ball over float gear, otherwise confine groundbait to the open-end feeder.

Loose feed is a better winter tactic, keeping very small amounts trickling in regularly, to try and stir the fish into a response. It's a good idea to rest an area which hasn't brought any bites after being fed for a long period. Often by trying something else, somewhere else in the swim and then reverting back to the first line, a sudden burst of activity will follow.

Bait Requirements

If you have bigger fish like carp in mind, then a bag of shop-bought boilies might be sufficient. Other big fish baits include sweetcorn and luncheon meat. But the chief requirements are likely to be as follows:

Maggots Several pints may be needed on a well stocked venue, where a good response might come from spraying a lot of bait over a medium range waggler rig. White, or bronze maggots are good for this approach. A smaller amount of red maggots ties in well with hemp and caster feed and for use with the open-end feeder. There's rarely need for more than a couple of pints of maggots in winter.

CASTERS For catches of small carp, or big bream, consider taking 3–4 pints of casters. Normal needs for a floatfishing session would be 1–2 pints and 2–3 pints for an open-end feeder approach.

HEMP A couple of pints of hemp is usually quite suffcient in summer, whereas a pint will meet most of your floatfishing requirements later in the season.

PINKIES A pint of mixed coloured pinkies is always a good standby bait, whether fishing float, or feeder gear. Notoriously fickle feeders like bream and skimmers often snap up a couple of red, or fluorescent pinkies, presented on a small hook.

SQUATTS Two pints of squatts may be needed for a long breaming session on the open-end feeder. These small feed maggots are good for

Above: Pinkies on a small hook frequently prove the downfall of fickle feeding bream.

Below: Small commons are sometimes confused with crucians, but crucians have no barbels.

holding fish, when fishing at distance. They can also be introduced into groundbait mixes aimed at tench and carp.

A few squatts introduced regularly in cloudy groundbait livens up cold lake swims. It's also worth trying them as loose feed when fishing close in. Their slow fall rate will stir big roach, perch and skimmers into action when the going is slow.

WORMS Lobworms and reds can be chopped into groundbait mixes at all times of the year when fishing for bream, tench and carp. A red worm tipped with a caster, maggot, or pinkie makes a superb bream bait. Worms also bring a response from big perch in clear, cold water. When used on the hook, induce some movement into them, by twitching float, or leger gear.

BREAD A good carp bait used in crust, flake, or paste form. It will also catch bream, tench, rudd and roach. Punched bread fished on smaller hooks is a good winter option.

BOILIES A standard bag of shop bought boilies goes a long way. There may be a need for greater quantities on larger venues. Fruit flavours tend to be successful in summer while savoury recipes pull more runs in winter.

MEAT Luncheon meat is a good carp bait, particularly on waters which haven't seen many boilies. Smaller cubes also take carp and tench, fished over groundbaited areas, or over a carpet of hemp.

GROUNDBAIT Plain bread crumb is fine with bread baits, or the open-end feeder. There are also many effective Continental lake mixes. Some cloud well, others fizz for ages on the bottom and even send floating particles to the surface. There are also some special recipes geared towards particular species like tench, bream and carp...and they do work!

In summer you may need a couple of kilo bags of Continental mixes and these can be further bulked out with three or four pints of plain brown crumb. A couple of pounds of groundbait in total should cover most winter trips.

RIGS

With no flow complications, stillwater float rigs often have lighter shotting down the line. In shallow and medium depths a lightly shotted waggler covers most possibilities both on-the-drop and on the bottom.

The only time to consider using a bulk, or larger dropper shot than No.8s is when small fish are a problem, or when drift pulls the float out of position.

Generally, even long range, bodied wagglers may only have two or three No.8s or No.10s spread out down the line.

Dropper shot are stepped up in numbers for deeper water so that it doesn't take ages for the rig to settle.

There are occasions when a larger dropper shot like a No.6, 4, or even 1 are positioned on the bottom, when laying-on for fish like tench at close range. This tactic produces lift bites, which are easy to hit.

Most insert wagglers are shotted down with spread No.8s, or 10s. As with all floats in the waggler family, the majority of shot still goes into locking the float.

There are times when fishing for small carp and rudd where no dropper shot are required. In this instance, a three or four foot tail is used below the float with a buoyant hookbait like dark casters, or floating maggots. But remember, the float needs to be feathered down in order to keep the terminal tackle landing in front of it.

In deep stillwaters, a bottom-end slider comes into the reckoning. At close range, use a stop shot several feet above the bulk, to help prevent tangles. For long range requirements, it's better to cast with a loaded slider resting on the lower bulk shot. This gains much greater distance, but again it's absolutely vital to feather the tackle down to avoid tangles.

Open-end feeder rigs should be fished on the loop method, described for river fishing in Chapter 5. In weedy waters the feeder may perform better set up paternoster style. Either system can be applied to leger tackle for distance fishing. A free running leger rig only tends to be effective at close range.

Long range legering, or feeder fishing may dictate the use of a shock leader to absorb the stresses of casting. This is a length of stronger line which is attached to the reel line, so at least three turns are on the spool when the leader is fixed to the end tackle, ready to cast. If you are feeder fishing with 3 lb or 4 lb line, use a 6 lb shock leader.

The quivertip is a very efficient bite indicator for long range legering. There's also a place for swingtips, which can be handy when fishing from heavily overgrown banks. It may not be

NIGHT LIGHTS

Starlites are a low cost way of illuminating the float at night. They're activated by breaking an internal seal which allows two chemicals to mix and produce the luminosity.

The glow lasts for approximately four hours and, depending on size, they're clearly visible within moderate range from the bank.

Various diameters of Starlite and their corresponding plastic tube holders are manufactured.

There are also floats with internal chambers in which the Starlite fits. That eliminates the need for the tubing.

The Starlite can also be used to illuminate the tip of a leger rod. If you tape one end of the tube holder to the opposite side of the tip to the rings, you'll have no problems with line fouling the Starlite.

Isotopes cost considerably more but last for years. They are normally fitted within the chambers of Swinger or monkey climber indicators.

Good organisation is essential for night fishing with everything laid neatly to hand. Never use powerful torches – a subdued penlight should be sufficient for re-tying rigs.

Remember that sound travels a long way in the dead of the night and it's imperative that you avoid upsetting your neighbouring anglers by clattering around the swim.

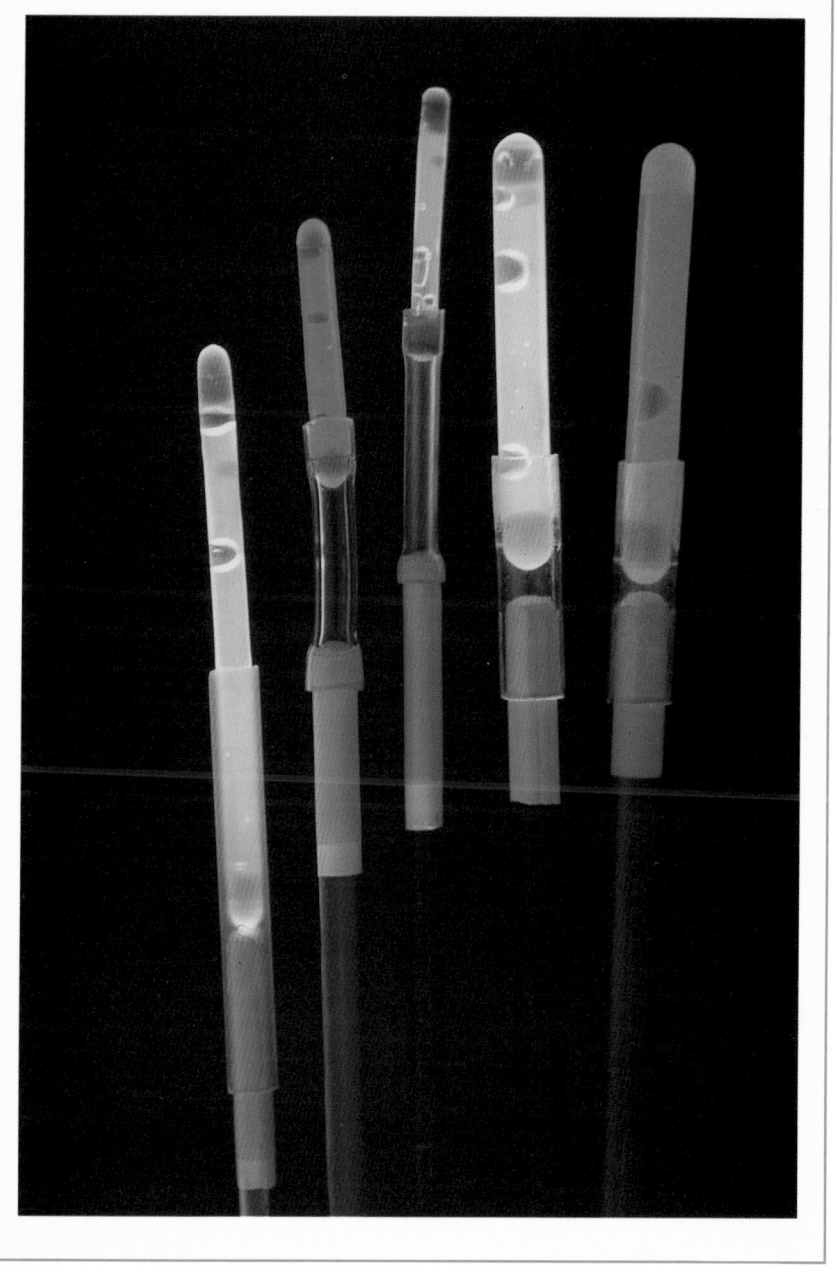

possible to position a quivertip correctly to one side in these spots, whereas the swingtip can be pointed directly out at the end rig.

Canal wagglers can also have a role on lakes and pits when fishing shallow water. These designs don't cause unnecessary disturbance as they land and are particularly effective in canal-like backwaters.

Insert wagglers fulfil the majority of stillwater float requirements, but straights are good in bad drift, when you want to anchor your hookbait hard on the bottom.

Remember here to sink your reel line. This can be done by over-casting, sinking the rod tip and winding several turns of line onto the reel quickly. Another option is to try flicking the line under, which should leave the float where it lands. This is done by flicking the rod top in the opposite direction to which the line is bowing in the drift.

Wagglers with long antennae are useful when trying to hit fickle bream and tench bites at close to medium range. These floats also ride rough water quite well.

In really choppy conditions, the bulbous sight tip on a windbeater float design is much more visible and helps stop the float continually dragging under.

CANAL FISHING

The massive network of canals offer enormous opportunities. Even grim looking industrialised pounds sometimes provide surprisingly good sport. Heavy boat traffic and busy towing paths pose problems in summer which means most canals come into their own in autumn and winter when specialist bait may be needed for consistent results.

Canals are popular with match anglers because they are generally fair venues and many swims are capable of producing winning catches. Indeed, every swim has at least some fish holding features in the shape of shelves on the near and far banks.

LOOK FOR BITES ON THE LEDGES

Noted feature pegs on canals include deeper piled banks, boat turning bays and marinas. There are also similar features to those you'd expect on some rivers, but more of them, such as locks and moored craft on the far bank. Obvious far bank features like overhanging foliage, wides, rush beds and streams running in, take on added significance. They provide havens for large shoals of fish, where they can keep away from the busy boat channel.

Many anglers avoid fishing the main channel until boat traffic dies away in the winter. But it is

possible to catch a lot of fish from this area during lulls between passing boats. The main channel tends to respond better to small, frequently fed baits, like squatts, pinkies and bloodworm. Some hard groundbait may also be required to try and hold the fish, because the bottom is so regularly disturbed.

But the most obvious lines of attack on these types of waterways are the near and far side ledges. A lot of small fish are usually caught early in a session, up and down the nearside shelf. Then normally a pattern emerges where the fish drift across the cutting.

On the far bank, very productive small fish areas are down the far shelf and further up it in featureless, shallow pegs. Larger fish normally hug thick far bank cover, or hole up where there is more depth, tight-in to far bank piling. They tend to push smaller fish away from these areas.

Small baits like squatts, pinkies, bloodworm, bread punch and hemp often score at close range and on the down side of the far shelf. They can also be used tighter across, if you think small fish are the main quarry. But caster is the No.1 bait where bigger fish are expected, followed by some bigger maggots.

Over recent seasons, chopped worm has become a potential match winning method and this is used in the boat channel, when traffic dies down later in the year.

Punched bread is a killing method on deeper, clear water canals, or where there is a lot of weed and few boats. Hemp combines well with this bait and is worth trying in its own right during warmer weather.

Because canals are popular and the water is often shallow, tackle needs to be fine and well presented for most methods. The only area where finesse may be sacrificed is the far bank. Good presentation is still essential, but many

Dave Coster reaches out with the long pole towards a boat moored on the far bank which is certain to attract bigger fish.

canals hold big fish like carp, chub and bream, so far bank caster rigs must be quite strong.

When selecting a canal swim, look for areas where the boats won't constantly disturb the quality fish. Wides, turning bays and streams running in, nearly always hold good bream, chub, carp and quality roach. Another good feature to search out is overhanging foliage which forces boats to keep away from the far side. Fish will normally hole-up underneath, or to the sides of this cover.

Permanently moored boats often hold a lot of fish. Select the derelict looking ones, or sunken craft as your first choice. Lived in, or well kept boats can also be good, but you don't know at first sight if you are going to get a lot of disturbance from people using them later in the day.

Deeper far bank swims are always a good bet and so are rush beds, which provide a haven and a lot of natural food. Deeper water areas above and below locks receive more flow and are better oxygenated. These spots are a bit too busy on hot summer days as boats queue to get through the locks, but are well worth a look later in the year.

Good nearside swims on canals are harder to define. Marginal weed growth, the inside of bends and deeper piled areas make a difference. But generally this area is pretty uniform and you will have to fish it to find out the potential.

On industrialised canal sections, buildings offer good cover and in winter may shield the water from cold winds. This draws fish from large areas...warm water outflows do likewise.

The really encouraging thing about canals is that the fish sometimes congregate in areas without any apparent holding features. This mystery element makes them all the more fascinating.

FEEDING TECHNIQUES

There are several useful accessories to help keep the feed tightly located. Small pouch pole catapults prevent too much feed going in and group it better. A bait dropper deposits neat bloodworm and joker on the bottom very precisely. Most important of all is the pole pot which clips onto the top section of pole. After being filled with loose feed or groundbait, it is pushed out across the canal and the contents tipped out where needed.

Loose feed and groundbait are both important methods for this type of fishing. It's wise to confine groundbait to one area of the swim to begin with, so you have other options if it doesn't work. Often cloudy groundbait is a very potent fish puller on canals. The only line it's never used on is the far bank caster area.

Harder consistency groundbait is used to get small baits like bloodworm, jokers and squatts to the bottom when boat traffic is on the busy side.

Groundbait is essential when fishing bread punch. Fine brown crumb, white punch crumb and liquidised bread all have their day. A cloud groundbait often gets a squatt line going. Some-

---

PLAN OF CAMPAIGN

Fishing several lines of attack is more important on canals than any other type of fishery for several reasons. A boat may steer off coarse and ruin one part of the swim for several hours. Or you may simply fish out one area. It's rare indeed to keep fish coming from the one spot all day.

There are five major areas to consider on the average canal swim. Up and down the nearside shelf, the boat channel, down the far shelf and tight to the far bank. The characteristics of your swim may eliminate one, or two of these areas. For example, boats could cut in very close because of a bend, or obstructive far bank feature. But you still want to try and feed at least two, or three lines.

But avoid spraying bait all over the swim! Feeding should be tight and precise, so it's essential to spend a long session on the plummet to pinpoint the shelves where loose feed and groundbait needs to go.

You could find a particular method like loose feeding squatts will cover a couple of lines anyway. These small maggots tend to scatter, so if you are catapulting them across the canal, they might well feed the area up and down the far shelf. It's still possible to fish one extremity of this feed area, leaving the other section for later in the day.

You may need to feed squatts in one, or two areas, punch crumb and hemp in another and casters on a further line. Feeding three or four baits in several areas regularly isn't possible all day.

The idea is to begin this way and to rotate tackle around the swim, until a couple of good catching areas have been established. After an hour you should know which these are and can forget the non-starters, or the spots which gave you just a couple of quick bonus fish.

By trying to narrow your feeding down into two, or possibly three areas, you can afford to lose one if a large boat disturbs that part of the swim. It also helps to rest areas in shallow water every now and than. This all helps to revive the bite rate when you go back over them.

times, you can also introduce the odd harder ball of groundbait with squatts, just to try and concentrate the fish – but continue with regular loose feed. Feeding hemp over squatts may pull larger roach.

Caster is usually fed with hemp. The magic seed complements big maggots well and often works on the hook in the deeper boat channel.

Bloodworms and jokers are cupped in neat later in the year when canals go clear. Remember that groundbait could kill a swim when the weather turns cold. Jokers can also be fed in leam, a fine binding clay which won't feed the fish off.

Sometimes, almost inexplicably, a heavy handed groundbait approach brings fading canal swims back to life. But there's an element of kill or cure. Introducing several large balls of heavy consistency groundbait, liberally laced with jokers, squatts, or bloodworm, brings instantaneous results or supresses the swim for ages. When this trick works, the fish seem to home in on the disturbance. Perhaps they associate the groundbait bombardment with natural disturbances. It can certainly set them rooting about in the swim looking for food.

BAIT REQUIREMENTS

The trick on canals is to take small amounts of a large selection of baits. Squatts are the only exception – in summer you might need two or three pints if there's a chance of bream.

By feeding squatts, you can try pinkies on the hook and as these rarely need to be fed, half a pint of mixed reds, whites and fluorescent maggots will be sufficient for a session. A half-pint measure of mixed colour, big maggots gives other hookbait options and a little to feed over to the far bank if casters don't work.

Casters are fed very lightly most of the time. Half a pint is normally enough. The only time you need to take 1–2 pints is if you are after carp, chub, or bream on a very prolific boundary.

A pint of hemp will also help to cover the far bank caster line and leave enough to try a hemp attack in the boat channel.

A kilo bag of groundbait is more than enough for any method. It's very rare to need to feed more than half this amount in fact.

In winter, bread punch starts to work well. This is a very economical method. All you need is a couple of pints of crumb feed, or half a liquidised loaf and a few slices of fresh white bread.

The most expensive canal bait is bloodworm

Canal vitals – pinkies, squatts and hemp. The fine textured groundbait is a special canal formula with brown crumb added.

and jokers. But on most venues a quarter-pint of worm for the hook and one pint of jokers for feed, will catch a lot of fish. Some canal regulars take a pint of larger bloodworm if they know bigger bream are on the cards. If jokers are going to be fed over two lines, the maximum requirement is two pints...and that's on a prolific water.

The chopped worm method is worth considering in winter. You may need a pot of lobworms and a couple of containers of small reds. The worm is cupped in, usually a couple of larger lobworms and up to a dozen smaller red worms, at irregular intervals. If the going is tough, fish may keep responding with the introduction of just a couple of finely diced reds every now and then.

If you're after big fish like carp and tench, sweetcorn, luncheon meat and boilies can be effective, usually fished over to far bank cover.

RIG STRATEGIES

Running line waggler rigs are very effective on canals. These are used on soft actioned 11, or 12 foot rods, with fine lines. This is really miniature waggler fishing. Short, streamlined, all-balsa caster and squatt wagglers may only take a couple of BB locking shot and very small No. 11, 12, or 13 dropper shot. Small No. 7 and 8 Styl weights also work well.

The soft actioned rod has two purposes. It enables hooklengths as fine as 0.06mm in diameter to be used if the going is tough. Forgiving, through actioned rods also cast light gear further and more accurately.

There are several reasons why running line waggler tackle should never be ignored. The long pole can spook fish on shallow, clear canals, unlike a waggler rig – as long as you are not too heavy handed on the cast. It's also easier to feed very regularly with a light rod by positioning it between the knees after the cast, while you catapult some bait out. Clearly, it's much harder to master regular feeding with a long, heavy pole in your grasp!

Running line tackle makes it possible to cast around the swim to pick up bonus fish. It will also long trot with the current when locks are in operation.

Generally, the waggler scores towards the far bank of canals, fishing down, on, or up the far shelf. Fish can be taken off the bottom when fishing small baits like squatts, but the best approach with casters and maggots is to present the bait well over-depth.

Nearside canal lines are usually covered by the pole. Very close in this is fished to-hand style and by using heavier capacity floats, it is possible to extend this method to four or five metres when speed fishing for small fish. But conditions must be right for long lining and immediately tackle control suffers, most canal anglers switch to short lining pole methods and unship sections to bring fish in. A short length of line between the pole tip and float gives much better tackle control, particularly in windy conditions.

The long pole is also a very good canal method. There are all sorts of rig possibilities for catching fish both up in the water and on the bottom. The pole scores highly when very tight control of the bait is needed, or when some movement must be injected into the hookbait to induce bites.

The pole should be seriously considered when running line tackle pulls off position due to bad drift, or because the canal is running rather too regularly. Missed bites from small fish is another reason to reach for the long pole which is more positive on these occasions. It's also possible to bulk more weight down the rigs with this method, in order to get through small fish.

Long poles are very useful when big fish are tucked in tight to far bank features. Drop lightly shotted tackle quietly alongside the cover and a bite will often develop instantly.

Most pole rigs are used with an internal elastic shock absorber and this allows the angler to use finer diameter lines. This is a great advantage in gaining a response from shy fish. The elastic will enhance the performance of thin diameter lines, in a way that is not possible with running line tackle.

While the pole has advantages, it's best not to forget that waving a long pole about over very shallow water scares fish. The pole should always be manoeuvred carefully, trying not to splash the tip into the water. It's also a good strategy, once the tackle has been lowered into position, to move the pole tip away to the side of the float. If you can keep it to the left, or right of the feed area and quickly pull hooked fish in this direction, the swim will produce for longer periods.

Pole rigs are comprehensively covered in Chapter 10, but when thinking of using long poles on canals, it's vital to first check there are no overhead power lines in the vicinity. These are very common on canal venues and there have been some very serious burn injuries and fatalities. So, as the warning goes – look up, before tackling up.

Light feeder tackle scores on some wider canals where there is a good head of chub, big roach, bream and carp. This is usually fished to the far bank. Some canals also have streams and small rivers running into them and when these are carrying extra rain water, the feeder comes into its own.

Short quivertip rods, often referred to as wands, combine well with light leger tackle on many canals. They're used with quite fine lines in open areas, or with stepped up tackle when fishing to features. These through-actioned rods absorb a lot of punishment and some big fish have been landed on them, including carp into double-figures.

Carp are stocked in many canals and have grown to specimen proportions. Twenty-pounders are quite common and odd 30 lb fish have been reported. This makes a specialist approach with stepped-up rods and Optonics a viable prospect and carp anglers are now looking at canals more seriously.

Although there will be plenty of instances where big fish and strong tackle come into the reckoning on canal venues, generally finesse is the name of the game. Always try to use the finest lines you feel safe with. Hooks should also be fine wire where possible and it's best to keep dropper shot on the small side. It also pays to scale down the diameter of reel lines. Many busy canals have an oily surface, due to spillage from boat traffic. Finer reel lines sink beneath the surface more readily than thicker ones, when better control is wanted with waggler tackle.

Canal towpaths are not normally very wide, so it isn't recommended to spread your gear around. Mountain bikes and fragile pole sections are an explosive mix.

Keepnets need to be staked out at both ends when constant boat traffic through the locks causes the canal to flow first one way and then the other. If you leave the bottom of the net untethered, it will swing through your nearside swim and kill sport stone dead every time a lock opens, or a boat passes.

Opposite top: **Miniature waggler fishing with a soft-actioned rod is very effective on canals.**

Opposite below: **Unloaded peacock waggler with lightweight cane insert.**

Below: **Improvised leg clamp serves as a keepnet or rod rest holder for impassible towpaths.**

UNDERSTANDING POLE FISHING

When you have learnt to catch fish consistently with rod and line and realised that good tackle control is crucial, you'll experience days when it's impossible to achieve the degree of presentation you'd like. Wind, surface tow, undertow, lack of flow and extra flow all conspire at one time or another to make running line fishing difficult.

Long poles swing the balance back in your favour, when awkward conditions defeat running line tackle. The pole offers you much tighter control of the float and allows you to do things which are not always possible with a shorter rod and long length of line. Furthermore here is much less line between a pole tip and the float and this opens up enormous possibilities.

With a long pole you can even tackle swims which are hazardous to rod and reel. Think of those days when you have reluctantly walked past a noted swim because it's covered in leaves, or clogged with weed. Good areas often have a lot of bankside cover which holds the fish resident, but which also restricts what you can do with a rod. The pole is different, you can add sections and drop the tackle into a tiny opening, or lay it out just inches from overhanging cover.

The pole also scores incredibly well when the fish are only half-heartedly pecking at hookbaits. It's possible to respond immediately to minute indications on a tiny and very sensitive pole float if the pole tip is directly above. The same bites would almost certainly be missed on running line tackle and you may not even see them at all on a thicker tipped float.

THE SPEEDY WHIP

Long poles allow tighter control of the tackle. They also make a huge difference when the fish are feeding freely and big catches are on the cards. Long lining, or fishing to hand is one of the fastest ways of accumulating big weights of small to medium sized fish.

The main advantage of fishing the long pole is that it puts you right over the fish! Tackle presentation can be spot-on and this reflects in more positive bites than you might expect with a running line.

Ideally you want your rig to be slightly shorter than the pole length so that fish can be swung easily to-hand.

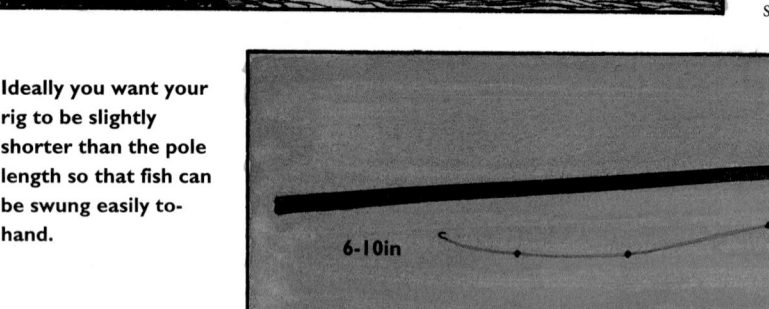

6-10in

When fully extended, all long poles will sag slightly. It's better to have a gradual even curve like this . . .

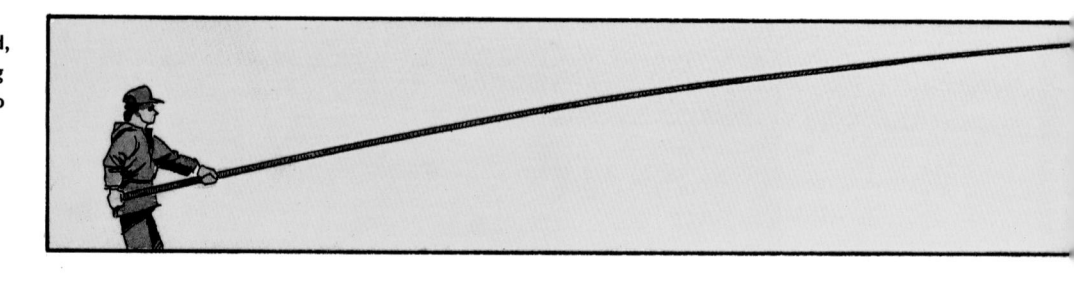

There's not a lot that can go wrong swinging the tackle out underarm, particularly if you use a bulk weight like a streamlined olivette some 14 to 24 inches above the hook. Tangles are scarce and you are getting the bait down to the fish fast.

This also applies to shorter poles, or whips as they are called. These range from just a couple of metres, up to seven metres in length.

Whips may be all telescopic for lightness, or part telescopic, so you can unship a bottom section, or two. They are primarily used for small fish. It's great fun whipping out a lot of gudgeon, small roach, perch, or bleak when nothing else is feeding. Experienced match anglers are very proficient at the method and sometimes amass surprisingly big weights.

CHOOSING THE RIGHT POLE

Budget priced poles may be made from glass fibre, or a composite mixture of glass and carbon. If you think back to when you were first choosing a rod, the same principles apply. Cheaper products are heavier and more bulky, but if you are unsure about the method, they'll at least provide an insight into what it's about and help you assess whether it's worth investing in a really top class model.

The mid-price range lies somewhere between £200 and £700 and it's possible to obtain some very good, long poles going up to 12.5 metres within this banding.

Top designs from 12.5 metres and anything up to 16 metres can cost into four-figures – so

Fishing tight against far bank cover.

while matchmen might be able to justify this level of extravagance, it's not essential for the average angler.

Overall, the more expensive poles offer superior rigidity, a slimmer diameter and are significantly lighter. Under competitive conditions, it's vitally important to gain those extra metres, because the fish tend to be pushed further out by heavy angling pressure. Pleasure anglers rarely have to fish to such extremes, because there is generally less bankside disturbance and the fish are not as well educated, if you steer clear of regular match lengths.

Having said that, it's still wise to purchase the longest pole you can afford. This isn't the contradiction it seems, because longer poles do offer more options. You may not need to fish the pole fully extended that often, but a spare couple of butt sections positioned ready on the bank can come in very useful. If a really good fish runs away from you. The quick witted angler can add a section and perhaps keep in touch with the fish.

A longer pole also comes in useful for chasing good fish across to the far bank of small rivers and canals. The better samples often lay under far bank cover and you can have a go for them.

There's more of a case for spending more on a longer pole if you know the venues you are going to fish require it.

Really you only need top-of-the-range extra-long poles if you intend competing in matches and at top level.

In this situation bank-side disturbance and people watching can push the fish well out.

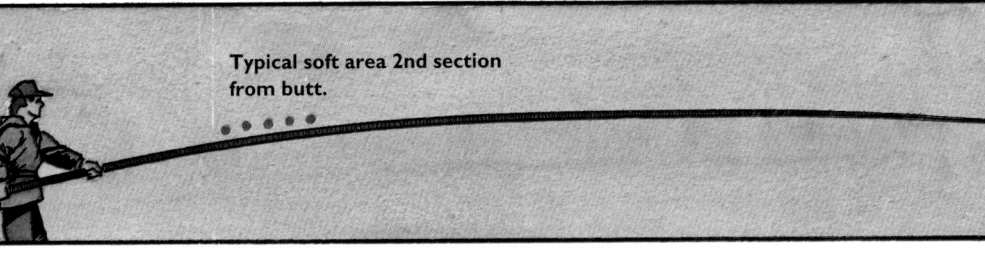

Typical soft area 2nd section from butt.

. . . than a pronounced sag at the butt end. If I tried to set the hook with this model, the bend on the lower section would transmit down the pole's length and bounce the tip all over the place.

ROLLERS AND RESTS

There are several useful devices which protect the pole from damage when fishing over rough terrain and also aid smoother handling.

The first priority is to obtain a good pole roller. This is positioned several yards behind your fishing position, so you can run several sections of pole over it, to reach the point where you want to break the pole down.

Apart from lifting the lower sections off the ground and keeping them clean, the roller also reduces strain on the middle sections and eases the pole back smoothly. This is vital if you have a fish on, because any jerky movements might pull the hook out.

A roller is not quite as essential if you are only fishing the pole at short to medium lengths. But if you drop the butt section its base will get damaged over hard ground. As a precaution, fit a protective base plug, or pole joint protector which will cushion any accidental impact, or even allow the base of the pole to be run along the ground if it's not too bumpy.

Right: **Wide gape pole roller.**

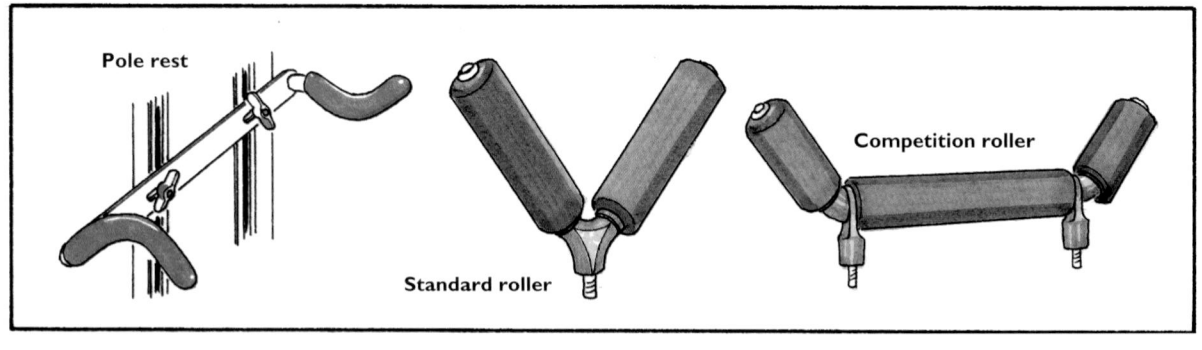

Pole rest

Standard roller

Competition roller

You may also find the fish tend to move just beyond your initial feeding range, after you've caught a lot. The last hour of a session can be really productive if you add an extra pole section.

But the most important factor behind getting the longest pole you can afford, is that it will often be better at shorter lengths, than shorter models when fully extended. An 11-metre pole will probably fish well up to ten metres, then become a little sloppy when fully extended.

If you want a good 11-metre pole, you are likely to find a 12, or 12.5-metre model much better when reduced to around the 11-metre mark, by leaving the butt section off.

Another important consideration when choosing a pole is to think about spare parts. Check with the tackle dealer about availability. You don't want to wait months if you need to replace a section, or want extra top sections.

Some mid-priced and most top of the range long poles come with an extra three or four section top kit as a spare. You can also fit different strength shock absorbers as back-up, should you need to change to lighter, or heavier tackle. Most experienced pole anglers end up with several top section kits, fitted with a diverse range of internal elastic systems to cover every eventuality.

HANDLING TECHNIQUES

When you first begin fishing with a long pole, you may find it's difficult to feed groundbait. A very helpful aid here is a pole rest. If you have a solid tackle box, there are special pole rest runners which bolt on the side. These allow a rest to be slotted in and angled at exactly the right position to keep the pole tip just above the surface after the butt section is located. There are also special rests which fix on external adjustable leg kits like the Octoplus system.

The secret of good pole handling is to keep everything smooth and unhurried, both as you manoeuvre the pole into position and bring it back, hopefully with a fish on. By trying to be too fast when fishing a short line, you risk cartwheeling the tackle into impossible tangles around the pole tip.

When a fish is hooked it should be brought up in the water, or steered to the left, or right of the shoal, before attempting to bring the pole

back. This prevents other fish from being frightened away from the feed area.

If you are confident that you can bring the pole in smoothly, it's possible to keep the pole tip above water. But if you can't at first stop the pole tip from bumping up and down as you retrieve it, try submerging the top two feet of pole in the water and this will help to cushion any bumpy movements.

It's easy to keep the float under tight control in calm conditions, but in gusting side winds the pole tip bounces about alarmingly, pulling the float off course. If this is happening you may have to slightly lengthen the amount of line between the pole tip and float. If things are really bad, you can also try steadying the pole by holding the butt between your legs and sit on the last foot of the butt, (still supporting the pole with your hands.)

Another good rough weather trick is to submerge the last couple of feet of the pole tip. This loses you a split second on the strike, but keeps plenty of bites coming by keeping the float still.

Most anglers hold poles up to 10 metres long with one hand, locking the pole under their elbow and supporting it on one knee. If wind, or a longer pole is making this a strain, try sitting

Above: **Unshipping with an unhurried, smooth action to avoid bumping off a small fish.**

Left: **Lightweight poles are no problem to hold for long periods using this relaxed grip.**

Feeding with the pole gripped between the legs.

WATCH FOR WORN JOINTS

Most poles have put-over joints. These are easier to unship and locate together, because the lower section fits inside the one above. These joints have slow tapers and come apart smoothly, so little can go wrong.

But watch for signs of wear on the sections you unship most often. When short lining, this is normally the third or fourth section down. The part which will wear most is the male half of the joint. If you can see the base cloth on which the carbon is layered showing through, the joint needs building up.

For bad examples of wear, brush on some carbon build-up liquid then rub it down so the joint stays smooth. For minimal signs of wear, or as preventative action, finer carbon sprays are certainly better. Most big tackle shops will advise on how to use these and may even undertake the work if you are unsure of what to do.

The other type of take-apart pole has put-in joints. Here the upper sections fit into the ones below. This type of joint is a little less smooth to unship when the pole is new, as it's more parallel and may require a little rubbing down with some fine wet and dry paper to begin with. Carbon sprays also help to keep these joints smooth running.

Telescopic poles sometimes need a

Where the upper section fits over the lower one, it's called a put-over pole. These models are popular with match anglers when smooth unshipping and speed are essential.

Worn male sections of joints which push in too far will need attention.

When upper sections fit inside lower ones the pole is referred to as a put-in model. This design can be stronger but less smooth, or more difficult to unship.

One or more coats of pole joint protector are applied, depending on the amount of wear.

little attention after a lot of use. You may see sections beginning to protrude further as they wear. If you take the pole apart from the butt and finely spray the lower ends of each section, the treatment should last for a season before the process needs to be repeated.

Grit and damp are the main enemies of the pole. Always try to clean your pole up after an outing. If sections remain wet and dirty, they will often seize-up during the next outing. It's very difficult to separate jammed sections and heavy handling can cause damage. A spot of furniture polish rubbed into male joints every now and then is a good preventative move.

Spray worn or damaged pole joints with a carbon restoring solution.

---

more sideways on and rest the butt section over both knees, steadying the pole with one hand in front of your knees and anchoring it with your other hand positioned slightly behind you.

Fishing to hand with short poles is a one-handed operation. The same technique with longer poles is best accomplished by supporting the butt between your legs and again sitting on the last few inches of the butt section. The pole is further supported with one, or two hands.

FLICK TIPS AND SHOCK ABSORBERS

Short poles, or whips are designed for small fish and should always be used with flick tips. These have a better action to help cast light tackle out

and act as a cushion if slightly better fish are hooked. A flick tip is also marginally more responsive on the strike and you'll hit far more bites by using one.

Flick tips are speedy when you're trying to accumulate large catches of small fish on the long pole, using small baits like squatts and bloodworm, or when trying to connect with lightning fast bites.

But it's advisable to use an elastic shock absorber for most of your longer pole fishing. You won't loose so many bonus fish and can in fact set your sights on catching some surprisingly large specimens.

The best and least tangle-prone shock absorber set-up is internal. The elastic is run

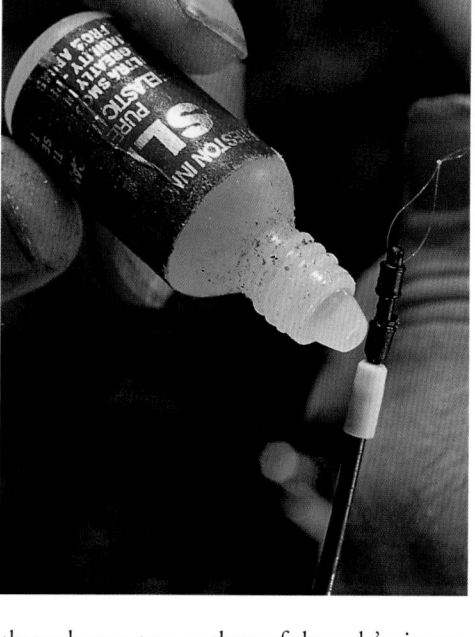

Left: Lubricating the internal elastic.

through one, two or three of the pole's tip sections. To do this, you'll need an elastic threader, PTFE bush, elastic/line adaptor, base bung and, of course, the elastic.

The hollow pole tip is cut back, to fit an inter-nal or external bush. This is vital, because being made from self-lubricating PTFE it will keep the elastic smooth running and prevent friction burn. Internal bushes may require slightly more of the pole tip to be trimmed back. They are probably better for thicker grade elastics. External bushes will save you a few inches of pole length, if you're fitting a very fine diameter shock absorber.

The next step is to decide over how many sections you want the elastic to run. There are several grades and the strength of the elastic often dictates how much you use. Fine elastics are combined with very delicate lines down to 0.055mm. They will stretch an amazing distance, even with very fine lines, so often threading them through just the tip section of pole is enough. This would entail using a very small base bung, matching one up from the wide range Stonfo produce.

Using a wire threader – Diamond Eye ones are easiest to use – the elastic is threaded through the bush end first and then pulled out of the base of the pole section where it is knotted to the hook on the base bung. The elastic should be slightly tensioned before tying the other end to a connector. This device has a protective sleeve which is threaded onto the elastic first. By removing this from the connector you will see the attachment hole which the elastic is knotted through. It is then covered by sliding the sleeve back into place.

At the other end of the connector is another sleeve which slides back to reveal a small crook. The line at the end of your pole rig is formed into a loop and pulled inside the crook and then securely locked in place by bringing the second sleeve back to its original place.

Once your elastic is installed in this manner there's one more essential task to perform on the bank. Although many pole elastics are ready lubricated, it's a good idea to smear some pole elastic lubricant over them before fishing. This guarantees many hours of smoothness and prevents water and surface debris from gumming up the works.

It is far more likely with medium elastics that you will want to fit up the top two pole sections with a longer shock absorber. Medium grades are used with slightly larger diameter hook-lengths such as 0.08 and 0.09mm mono-filament. You will, of course, be looking for better sized fish and may need to tension the elastic even more to set the hook. However, you will still need a lot of give in reserve, to stop good fish

Left: Generally it's best to use an internal shock absorber when long pole fishing. Use fine elastics (sizes 1-3) in just the tip section, and medium-to-heavy elastics in the top two sections.

Medium-to-heavy elastic set-up.

Fine elastic set-up.

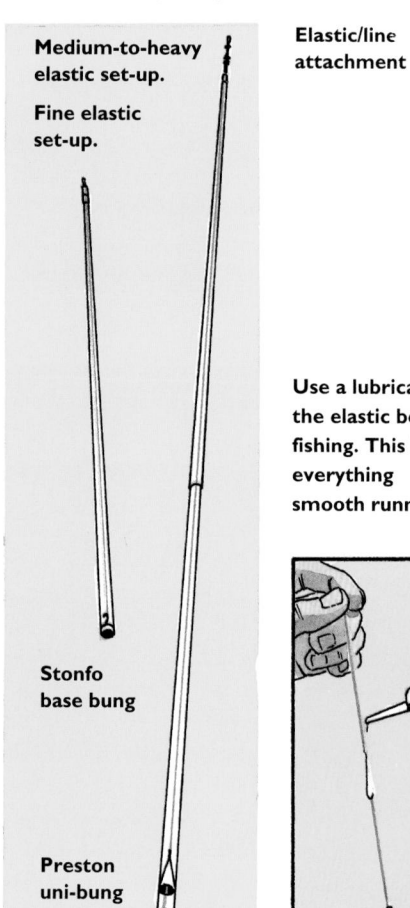

Stonfo base bung

Preston uni-bung

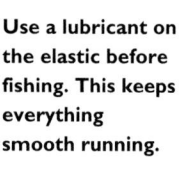

Elastic/line attachment

Use a lubricant on the elastic before fishing. This keeps everything smooth running.

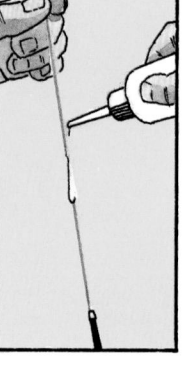

from smashing what is still relatively light gear.

The best base bung here is a Preston Innovations cone-shaped one, which can be cut to exactly the right size to fit up inside the base of the second pole section. If you are using a pole with put-over joints you will have to locate the bung several inches inside this second section in order to slide the third section on. These bungs have a nylon, or plastic tail, so you can still remove them.

It's now normal with heavy elastics to thread up two, or even three pole sections. The latter is an open water tactic when going for big fish like carp, tench and bream. In more confined areas you may have to compromise with tensioned elastic in two sections, to have a chance of getting big fish away from snags quickly.

Plenty of pole elastic lubricant should also be smeared on two and three section set-ups. If you are catching good fish, it also doesn't hurt to re-lubricate the shock absorber two or three times during the session.

Getting the tension right in the first place is a matter of trial and error. If you are bumping fish on the strike the elastic may need tensioning more. Tensioning may have to be varied depending on how the fish are feeding on any particular day. If you don't want to cut the elastic back, it is possible to buy elastic tensioners, or some base bungs incorporate such a facility.

FISHING-TO-HAND

With a flick tip you can fish to hand with a bulk weight, made up of grouped shot, or an olivette, set near to the hook. This helps swing out the tackle. But if the fish are up in the water, you can also use a strung out rig and flick it out, over-head, or from the side, utilising the pole's action.

On longer poles it's essential to use a low slung olivette to get the tackle out, but you can still put some finesse into the rig by using a long hooklength with two or three small shot spread evenly on it.

This method is best kept simplified when the fish are feeding well and one dropper shot will suffice with minimal line between the olivette and hook.

There are three main ways of taking fish on the short pole to-hand style. One is to position an olivette or bulk shot very close to the hook. This tactic normally applies to fish like gudgeon and bleak. Gudgeon are bottom feeders, so a classic rig would be a .75, or one-gram olivette set just 6–8 inches from the hook, with one No. 10 dropper shot 2–3 inches from the hook. The ideal setting here is to get the dropper shot just off bottom and the hookbait resting lightly on it. The float should have a heavy cane, or wire stem so it cocks quickly. The heavy olivette for such a short pole will also get the bait down fast. The float itself should be well dotted down. A cane, or nylon bristle is best for this.

Another good bulk rig is designed for up in the water work when after species like bleak. This entails using small streamlined balsa floats with no dropper shot, just a small bulk of No. 8, or 10 shot set 4–6 inches from the hook. These help to flick such a light rig out and allow depths of between one and four feet to be fished.

Small fish like bleak and gudgeon are normally avid feeders and this is one of the few occasions where you don't have to worry about fishing a bulk very close to the hook. Speed is just as important as presentation if you are going to amass a good catch.

Species like roach, perch and skimmers will rarely be fooled by such heavy weights placed so near to the bait. You may still require a bulk for speeding the bait down to the lower depths and for swinging the tackle out, but it needs to be pushed much higher up the rig. In order to balance the tackle, two or more small No. 10, 11, or 12 shot may have to be strung out evenly to the hook to give the hookbait a natural fall over the last few feet of its descent.

You can try grouping the dropper shot closer to the hook and shove the olivette down if the fish are coming thick and fast, but often they'll wise up and the bulk may have to be pushed

Below: **Basic bottom fishing format**

Below right: **Up in the water rig**

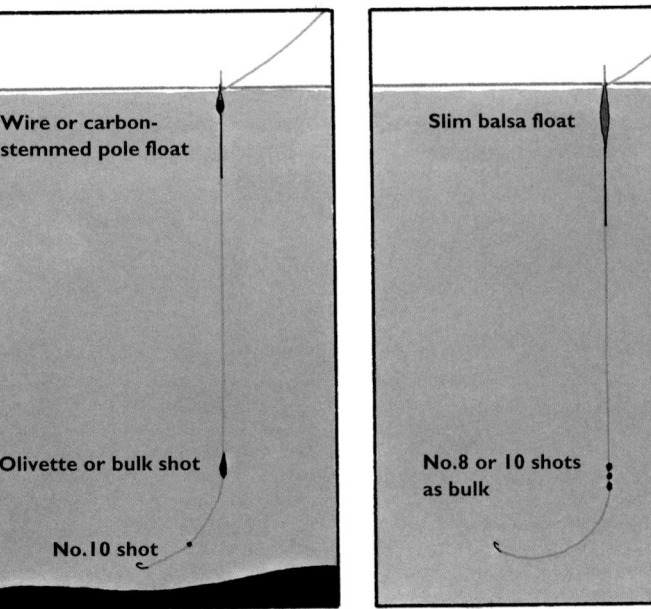

Wire or carbon-stemmed pole float

Olivette or bulk shot

No.10 shot

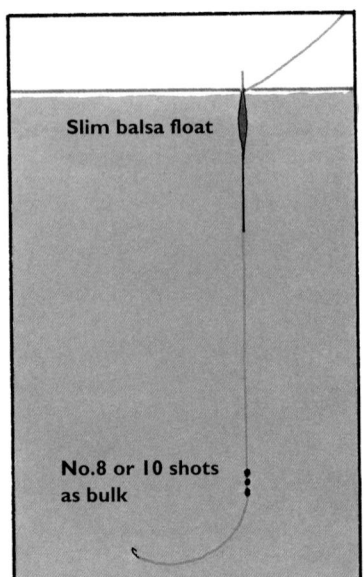

Slim balsa float

No.8 or 10 shots as bulk

three feet up the rig and the small shot below shuffled around until positive bites materialise.

The third major way of catching on the short pole, is with strung out shotting, or Styl weights. The idea is to cover the whole depth of the swim, often taking fish on-the-drop.

This is achieved by evenly stringing small shot or Styls from the float to the hook, or by starting them from mid-depth down to the hook. The latter formation may require the last few dropper weights to be spread a little further apart. This method suits fine presentation with baits like bloodworm, bread punch, pinkies and squatts. It's a good way of taking mixed catches of perch, roach, skimmers, bleak, rudd and even gudgeon once the rig has settled.

With longer lining techniques, bulk weight size is regulated by the length of pole being used, the depth of water and the prevailing conditions. Generally olivette size is determined by what you can comfortably swing out to the desired distance. Anglers visiting Ireland and Denmark may step up to really big bodied pole floats carrying as much as 8 to 14 grams for better speed, control and distance.

Regular feeding is crucial when fishing to-hand rigs. Often regular cloudy groundbait is combined with loose feed for up in the water rigs. A medium consistency groundbait may be used as a carrier to get small offerings like bloodworm, jokers and squatts down to the bottom and then break up quickly. Heavy groundbait mixes, holding a lot of feed like casters are used when after bigger fish and really big catches on the long pole to hand.

Long Pole Fishing

Most long pole fishing incoporates a short line between the pole tip and float. Several pole sections are run back behind your fishing position, so the pole can be broken down to swing the tackle in to hand. The length of line varies in relation to still and flowing water.

It's easier to connect with shy bites if the length of line is minimal, but obviously more line has to be used on flowing water, basically to

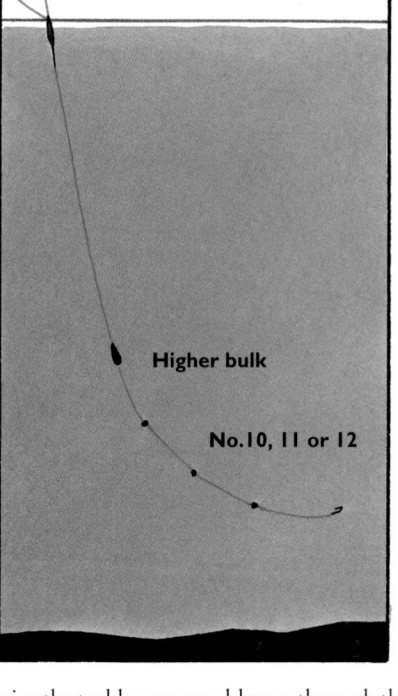

Higher bulk

No.10, 11 or 12

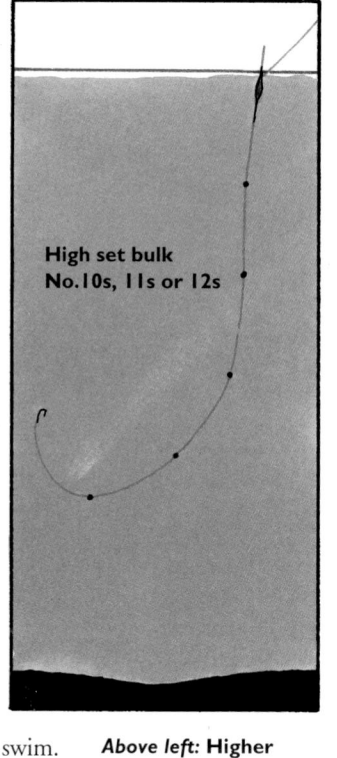

High set bulk
No.10s, 11s or 12s

give the tackle a reasonable run through the swim.

Long pole/short lining methods score well when the fish are less active, or when conditions make running line rigs less effective.

Apart from giving you superb tackle presentation, short lining techniques also allow the hookbait to be teased in several ways to tempt bites. The tackle can be manipulated very closely with your feeding, lifting the bait and letting it drop again each time you introduce more feed. With experience it's possible to work your tackle perfectly in unison with loose feed.

The hookbait can also be inched back against surface tow. This tactic works because often the lower levels will be going the other way. Your loose feed may appear to be travelling in the same direction as surface drift, but nine times out of ten, it will actually start to change direction as it hits the undertow.

Another very effective long pole bite inducing device, is to fish the rig set well over-depth and to twitch the bait along the bottom, backwards and forwards over the feed area. This works particularly well with baits like bloodworms and red-

Above left: **Higher bulk rig.**

Above: **An evenly strung shot or styl rig**

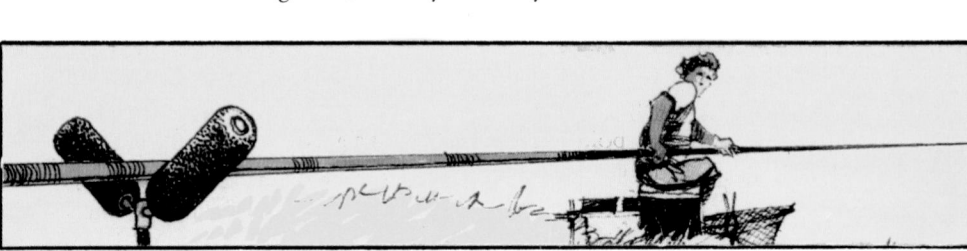

Pole rollers allow several pole sections to be slid back smoothly and in one go. They also prevent damage to the pole over rough ground.

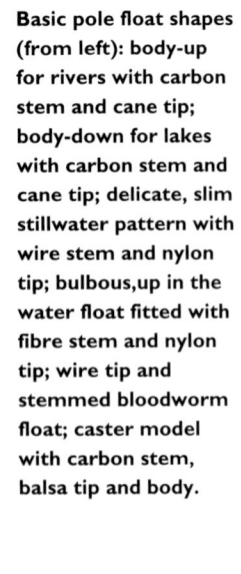

Basic pole float shapes (from left): body-up for rivers with carbon stem and cane tip; body-down for lakes with carbon stem and cane tip; delicate, slim stillwater pattern with wire stem and nylon tip; bulbous,up in the water float fitted with fibre stem and nylon tip; wire tip and stemmed bloodworm float; caster model with carbon stem, balsa tip and body.

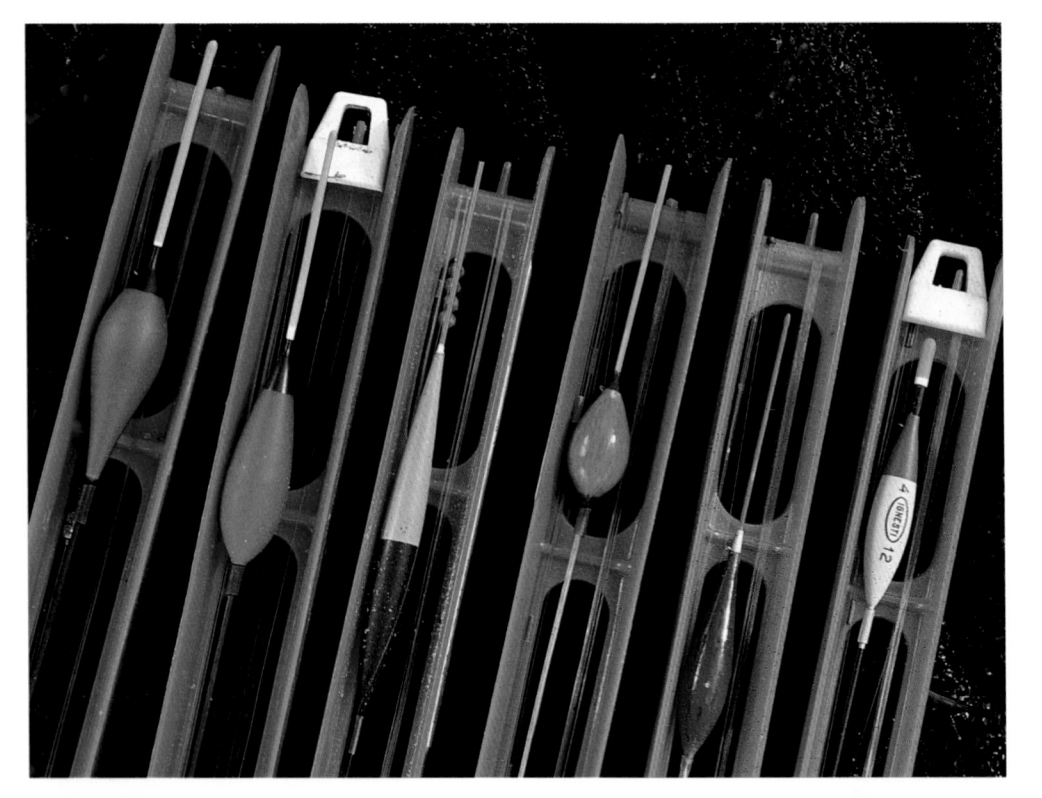

Small pole floats for tackling shallow ledges on the far bank.

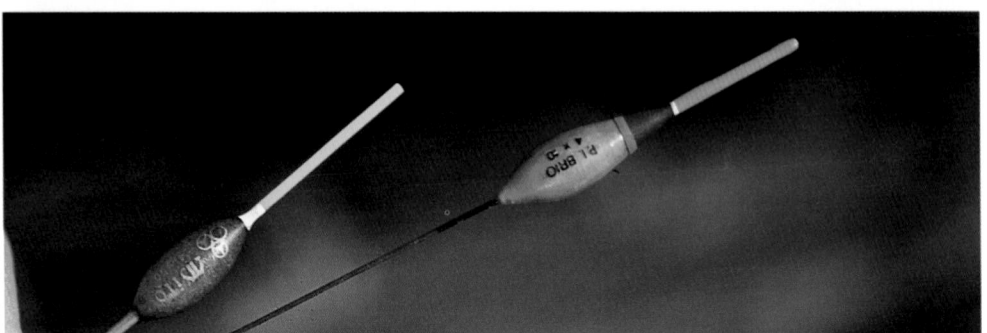

worms. Perch can't resist this movement and it also brings surprising results with species like roach, tench and bream.

On running water, the long pole can be used to slow hookbaits right down, even to a standstill and at distances well beyond the capabilities of rod and line. This is a particularly good winter tactic and has great possibilities when extra water is trotting the tackle through too fast.

LONG POLE RIGS

Most anglers design their own highly individual rigs, but there needs to be a starting point. The following tried and tested tackles will catch you a lot of fish and cover most situations you are likely to come across:

LAKES AND GRAVEL PITS
RIG 1: ON-THE-DROP

Most stillwater pole floats with a pronounced body shape have a gradual taper towards their fine wire, nylon, carbon, or cane tips. These body shapes are referred to as body-down.

On-the-drop rigs can be fished at full depth in shallow swims, or well off bottom in deeper water. But the latter tactic only tends to be productive during the warmer months when the fish are very active.

Strung micro shot, or Styls are best for this type of fishing to give the hookbait a slow fall. Floats are on the small side, usually no heavier than 0.4 of a gram. The best float designs have cane, or carbon stems, so they cock in line with the slowly falling end tackle. Carbon tips are more sensitive for smaller baits, while nylon tips

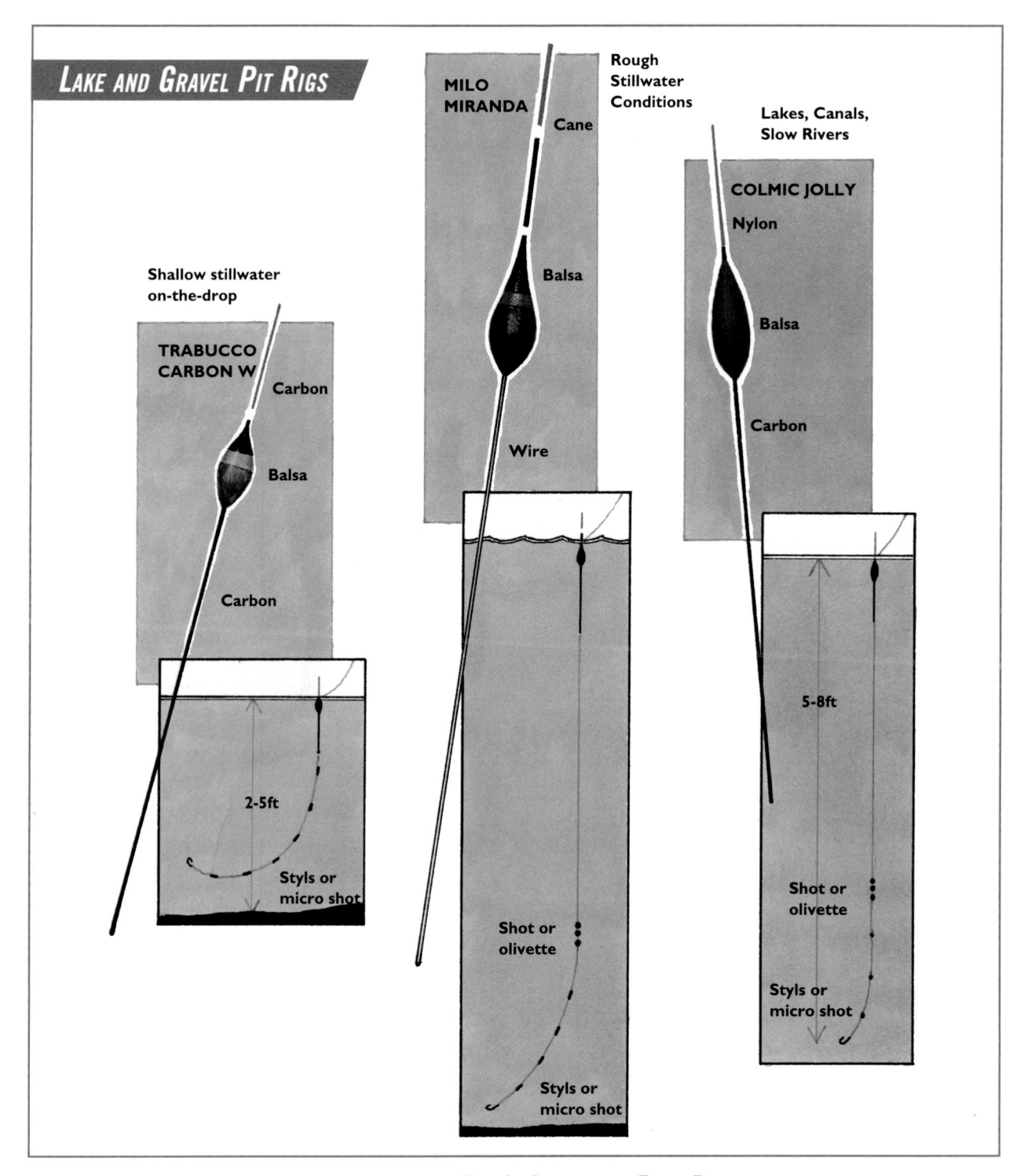

LAKE AND GRAVEL PIT RIGS

Shallow stillwater on-the-drop

TRABUCCO CARBON W

Carbon

Balsa

Carbon

2-5ft

Styls or micro shot

MILO MIRANDA

Cane

Rough Stillwater Conditions

Balsa

Wire

Shot or olivette

Styls or micro shot

Lakes, Canals, Slow Rivers

COLMIC JOLLY

Nylon

Balsa

Carbon

5-8ft

Shot or olivette

Styls or micro shot

---

are used for larger baits like maggots and casters.

The floats' weighting can be evenly spread for deeper on-the-drop fishing, (4–8 feet), but it's better to group small weights at half to one-inch intervals halfway down the rig for very shallow work, spreading a couple of tiny dropper shot at wider intervals down to the hook. This still gives the tackle a slow fall if controlled on a tight line, but most importantly, it stops too many tangles.

RIG 2: STANDARD FULL DEPTH

A bulk weight is needed here, but if the swim isn't too deep, strung shot, or Styls are used slightly spread below half depth, to slow the bait down over its last few feet of fall.

There's a wide choice of float sizes here, depending on depth. Floats in the 0.3 to 0.75-gram carrying capacity are used in depths down to eight feet, depending on conditions. Deeper

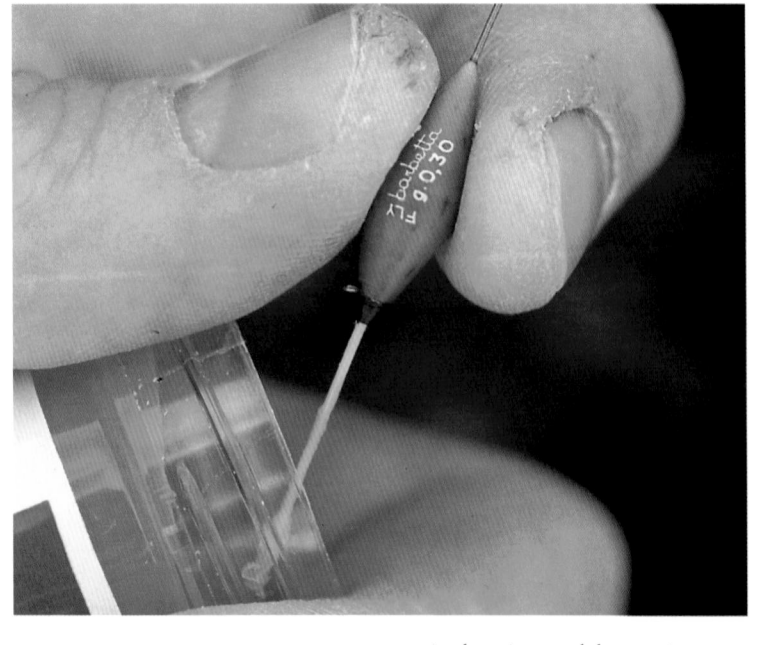

Greasing the sight tip helps make it stick in the surface tension if the shotting is too precise and the float is tending to submerge.

Styl pinchers are essential to pick up these tiny weights and fix them accurately.

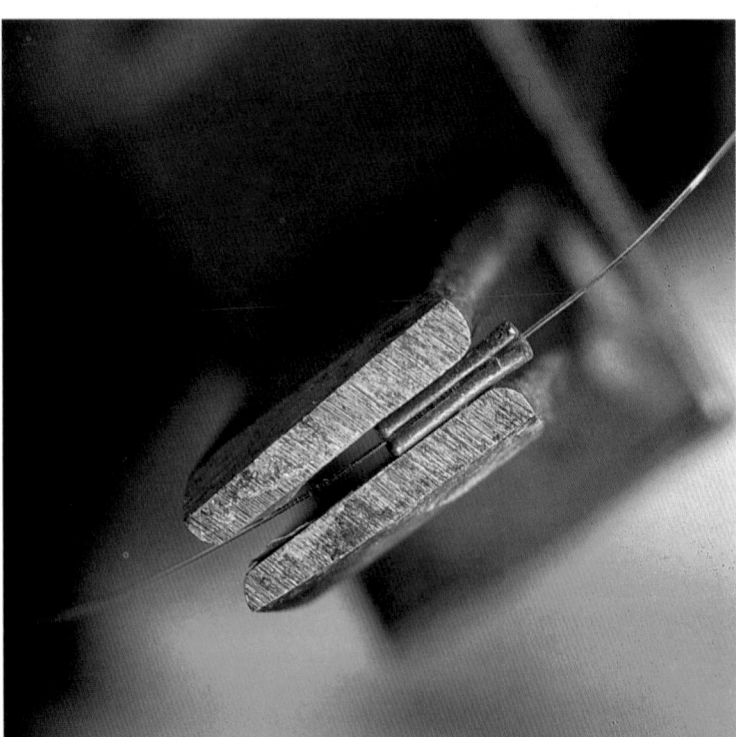

water may require heavier models carrying anything up to two grams.

Body-down floats are correct for these rigs, stems should be carbon, or wire. Tip material may be wire or carbon for small baits like bloodworm. Nylon is better for supporting maggots, casters, bread punch and redworms.

Below a spread shot, or olivette bulk, try and use several small strung Styls, or micro shot, so the hookbait falls more naturally over the last few feet of its descent.

RIG 3: BIG FISH

The long pole can account for big fish like tench, bream and carp. A heavy elastic shock absorber is used with 0.10 to 0.15mm hooklengths. Hooks should also be strong and in some situations may have to be forged.

In order to balance this stepped-up tackle, a good degree of presentation is achieved by keeping floats on the small side. These are weighted down with small shot, either strung out, or partly grouped and strung. It's very important to use soft micro shot, because these move if a good fish bolts into weed cover. It's better they slide up your line rather than breaking it.

Normally large offerings are used for this method like double casters or maggots, even sweetcorn, so the float tip needs to be quite buoyant. Thicker nylon, or fibre bristles are best. It's also possible to purchase specialist balsa tipped floats for this type of fishing.

Use body-down float shapes in calm conditions, a body-up design may be better if the rig needs to be held very still in bad drift. Cane or carbon stems are best, although wire can be used in drift.

CANAL

RIG 1: DEEP WATER/MAIN CHANNEL

Small olivettes, or closely grouped small shot can be used to get the bait down quickly. One or two dropper shot will cope with small fish, but the bulk may have to be moved up and some more micro shot evenly spread below to fool larger roach and skimmers.

Float shapes should be slim, or body-down. The float should be stable, so wire, or carbon stems are required. Tip material depends on the baits being used. Use wire for bloodworm and squatts, carbon replaces this if rough conditions are swamping the float and is also applicable to baits like punch, hemp and pinkies. Nylon sight tips are better for bunches of bloodworm, chopped worm, maggots and casters.

Floats carrying from 0.03 to 1 gram are most used on this line.

RIG 2: SHALLOW/ON-THE-DROP

This is small float territory. Tiny floats carrying from just three No. 8 Styls up to 0.3 of a gram are mainly used with spread out micro shot, or Styls from size 7s to 9s.

The float can have carbon, cane, or wire stem material, depending on the rate of fall you want

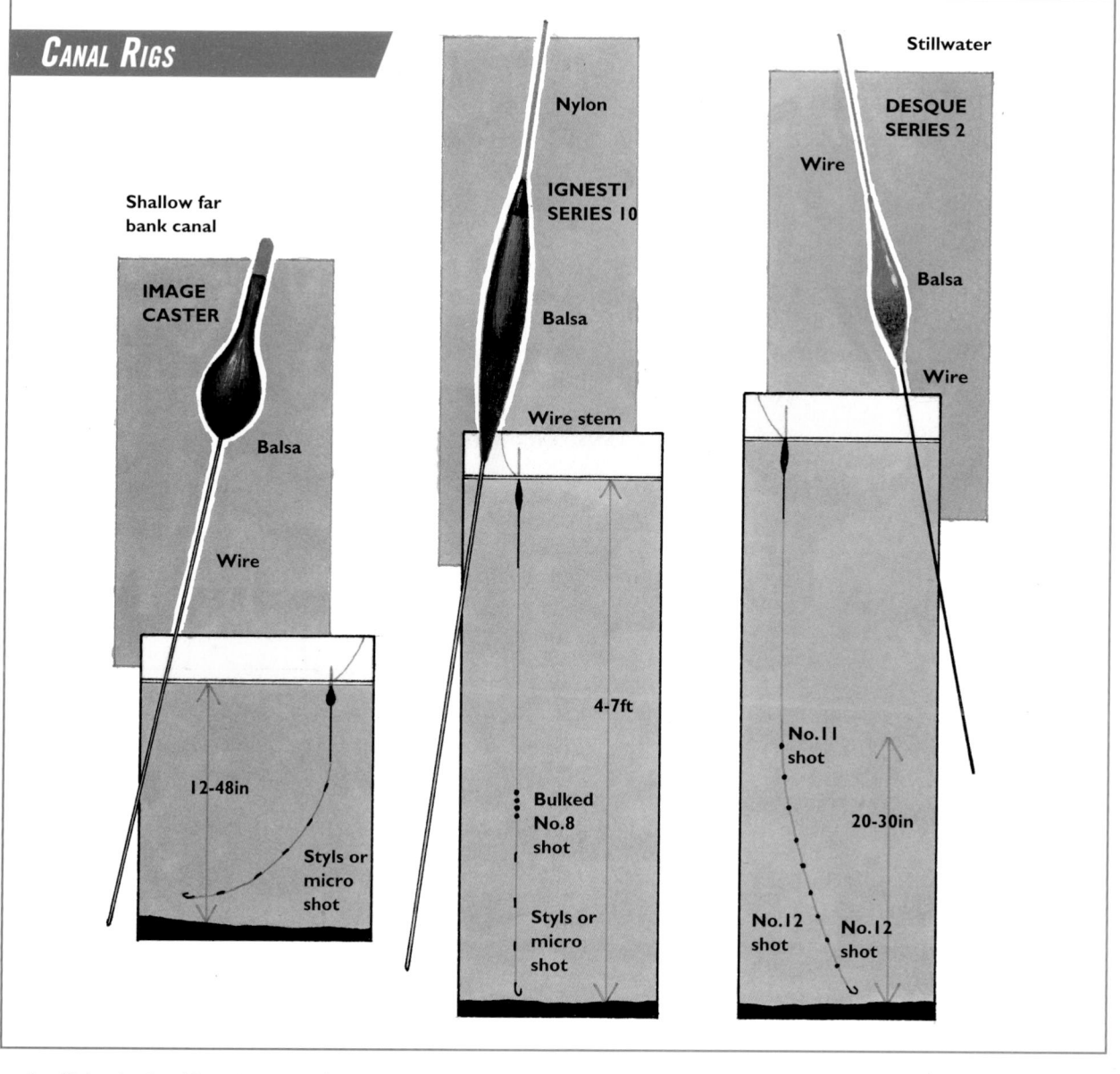

CANAL RIGS

Shallow far bank canal

IMAGE CASTER

Balsa

Wire

12-48in

Styls or micro shot

Nylon

IGNESTI SERIES 10

Balsa

Wire stem

4-7ft

Bulked No.8 shot

Styls or micro shot

Stillwater

Wire

DESQUE SERIES 2

Balsa

Wire

No.11 shot

20-30in

No.12 shot

No.12 shot

to instill in the hookbait. Tips can be wire, or carbon, but you may have to change to nylon, or balsa if conditions are windy, or the tow is bad.

Body shapes should be slim in calm conditions. A small body-up float may prove more effective if the canal is running a lot, or if there are bad side winds, otherwise use body-down shapes. Round bodies are also worth considering in bad winds.

RIG 3: FAR BANK/BIG FISH

This is again shallow water fishing so the float size should be on the short side and take minimal shot, or strung Styls.

Although the float may only be carrying three or four No. 8 Styls, or the equivalent in micro shot, its tip should be slightly thicker than nor-

mal. This helps visibility when fishing the pole at maximum length and the majority of times baits like casters and maggots are fished over-depth, so the tip should also be quite buoyant. Nylon, or balsa tipped floats are favourite. Stem material can be a short piece of wire, carbon or cane.

RIVERS

RIG 1: BULKED/TROTTING

An olivette is used, unless lack of flow allows a light float, then small shot can form a wider spread bulk, set below half depth. This latter tactic pulls the rig through better – utilising to full advantage what little current there is.

Classic body-up running water pole floats can be used, but round, or rugby ball shaped bodies

Pole River Rigs

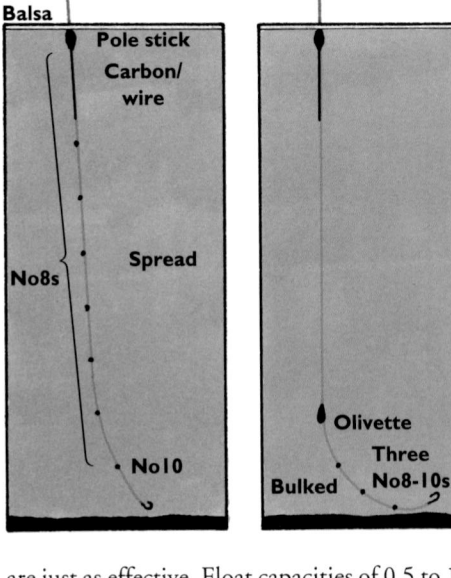

Balsa
Pole stick
Carbon/ wire
Spread
No8s
No10

Olivette
Three
Bulked No8-10s

RiverRigs

TRABUCCO CARBON Z

Carbon
Balsa
Carbon

4-12ft

Olivette

Micro shot

are just as effective. Float capacities of 0.5 to 1.5 are the norm, but in deeper, or faster water there may be a need to step up to 2-4 grams.

Wire, or carbon stems are best for this type of trotting work. The float tip would normally be nylon for most baits and flow rates, but more sensitive carbon, or wire can be introduced in lesser flows especially with smaller baits like bloodworm.

Dropper shot can be kept down to a minimum – 2 or 3 most of the time. No. 8s, or 10s are commonly used.

RIG 2: STRUNG/TROTTING

Similar floats to those above may be used, or more specialised Pole Sticks, which are basically more streamlined versions of the running line stick floats.

No. 8 or 10 shot, or larger Styl weights are evenly spread down the rig, usually tapering down in size slightly towards the hook.

RIG 3: HOLDING BACK

Round, or body-up floats tend to hold back well in flow without riding up out of the water. The tackle is controlled on a tight line and either held stationary, or edged through the swim at different speeds until bites materialise.

Wire stems are the most stable for this technique. Nylon is the best tip material.

Float sizes begin at 0.75 and move up to several grams in faster water. It is also a good idea to try over shotting lighter floats, if bites are difficult to connect with. The float won't sink if you hold it against the flow on a tight line.

The tackle should be fished over-depth and three or four dropper shot, (10s, or 8s) are probably about right.

INDEX